BEYOND

A Book of Poems
By
John Niemirovich

American Literary Press
Five Star Special Edition
Baltimore, Maryland

Beyond

Copyright © 2005 John Niemirovich

All rights reserved under International and Pan-American copyright conventions. No part of this book may be reproduced, stored in a retrieval system, or transmitted in any form, electronic, mechanical, or other means, now known or hereafter invented, without written permission of the publisher. Address all inquiries to the publisher. All opinions expressed herein are those of the author and do not, necessarily, represent those of the publisher.

Library of Congress
Cataloging-in-Publication Data
ISBN 1-56167-905-4

Library of Congress Card Catalog Number:
2005904867

Published by

American Literary Press
Five Star Special Edition
8019 Belair Road, Suite 10
Baltimore, Maryland 21236

Manufactured in the United States of America

Poet

A child, in awe of all I see and know,
Withdrawn from all the world in expectation,
I ply the meter of my pleading verse
That gently probes the universe for understanding.

Herein several of my innermost thoughts originally not intended for public perusal. But now constrained by doubtful circumstances to publish, it is hoped that only those beyond a critical age are moved to that degree of inquisitiveness which would intrigue them to the point of purchasing, upon the market, this small book of poems.

—John Niemirovich

Beyond

To Tony Niemirovich

When friends are gone and speak no more,
It's sad to think of all unsaid;
Though many words were passed between,
They never quite expressed enough.

Wonder

I know the world is filled with wonders,
But wonder of wonders is the number
Who know as much with much less wonder.
I wonder why I wonder much too much?

The Flight of Light

Of all the many events occurred
There naught remains but now. Though time is one,
Yet place of time is scattered far and wide
Allowing light its journey long until
Events that once were far are now at hand
And all is intertwined into the universe.

The Beach of Time

We, thoughtful travelers, walking staid upon
The beach of time that stretches ever on,
Do stamp our prints on smoothed sand
Whose countless grains have countless prints erased.

John Niemirovich

Spring

Spring is here again to share its mirth;
I tried with all my might to watch its birth,
But try to watch and wait as much I could,
The grass has greened and sprouted overnight.

The Weaver's Clue

When I bethink myself how fragile is
The fabric life has chosen itself to clothe,
How swirling dust was raised and formed in shape
And then imbued with lofty spirit proud,
The marvel of form and shape, though great, becomes
A lesser miracle to point the way unto
The awesome mystery we call our soul.

A Question

If all the stars that light the universe
Obey immutable laws in every place,
Where birth and life and death of each becomes
Identical, then who can say that suns,
Innumerable and formed by force of gravity,
A force unique, must live by laws apart?
Ought not the neighboring cosmic space
Where planets endure astral orbiting
Be governed by these permeating laws
And worlds and beings in profusion exist?

Beyond

A Blushing Flower

A flower small along a trampled path
In solitary splendor blushed in bloom
And fluttered to the slightest passing breeze,
But not a single traveler saw its pride.

A tearful eye bespoke its broken heart
As gaiety and joy of happy life
Departed from its tiny petals rare,
While slowly withered away its comeliness.

The gently falling rain in vain did balm
Its aching, searing, lonely heart unloved;
An understanding sun could never quite
Bestow a warm and happy festive mood.

Be fair apprised my unrequited love,
Or else I am that hapless flower above.

The Reach of Man

If anything be perfect it endures forever,
And never ceases its intended function.
The universe its many stars in constant change,
In part, as seen by mortals limited scope,
Does follow ephemeral path in nature's scheme.
Imperfect though as nature's laws may seem
Corrections abound where mortal minds do teem,
To wit: intriguing glimpse of immortality.

John Niemirovich

Amen

Never mind the mad illusions rare
That capture fair, in limitless fantasies,
Your fired, intoxicated imagination;
We still must age and waste away to nil.

Lost Familiarity

And now that those of us who played their parts
In any one of life's innumerable dramas
Have left the stage for realms beyond our view,
Another page of life has turned aside,
And all they deemed familiar now is lost
Within the failing light of yesteryear.

Continuity

It seems that we who live upon this globe,
From dust arisen to life and thought,
Are but the mind and eyes of Mother Earth
Which look upon herself and to the stars.

We marvel all the while at wonders seen
Afar in chilly, endless, awesome space,
And at the many miracles at hand,
But seldom feel the oneness of it all.

Beyond

Illusion

What if, in all this mystery of life,
With which we struggle constantly to know
Yet seldom learn, it seems, but resignation,
The piquing knowledge came to us
While we were crossing to the great beyond,
That life was nothing more than sheer illusion?

Incredible Remembrances

When I was young, a million years ago,
I dreamed a million dreams of youthful joy
And never had a sober, chilling thought
Of where those happy days of warmth would lead.
But now the sunny days of yesteryear
Have gone and taken all their reverie,
I've nothing left but cold reality.
I wonder how I dreamed those soaring dreams?

John Niemirovich

A Long, Lost Friend Remembered

I saw a friend from ages long ago,
Whose features time had changed enough to mask,
Though momentarily, the face that once
I thought I knew as etched in timelessness.

I struggled a time in effort to recall
The many happy days we spent together
In sharing all we knew in days gone by,
The days we thought would surely last forever.

The past is mist, but dimmer still the dreams
We dared assume were meant for us alone
And must come true because our fervent faith
Was sure to guaranty our destiny.

In limbo lies our rare, unsullied dreams;
Perhaps to grace some other dreamers' faith.

Beyond

Harvest

Its splendid cycle repeated endlessly
Through ages numberless and days untold,
Bold autumn's swift approach is past again,
And winter's icy blast is felt in chill.

The trees are bare anew. The ground is strewn
With shriveled leaves that only days ago
Bedecked the spectral branches standing stark
In warm, translucent red and golden hues.

No bird to sing through warm sunny days,
No chirping, furtive cricket's serenade;
There nought remains of weary winter time
But drear anticipation next of spring.

Insulated Ego

I wonder if the body, which our soul
Has found on Earth a waiting residence,
Was meant to be included in the list
Of dire accountability to us
So any act or word we do or say
Extends to us as well as others, too?

John Niemirovich

The Dilemma of Quest

When mood shall move my sleeping psyche deep
And carry far awareness of the world—
This hectic world—to sense the power high,
That rules and regulates entirely
The most minute phenomenon unknown,
The dizzy height bestirs capricious yen;
I feign would snatch the fleeting imp of time
And hold it fast until it stirs no more
That I may know the peace that changes not.

The Long Journey Home

If you, of all the multitude that now
Reside upon the Earth, were born the first
And felt a stirring thought within your mind,
To seek the answers to your world about,
To whom and where would query carry you?

A Dreamer's Caution

A dream is rare enchantment sweet that far
Beyond the bounds of strife and earthly care
Does waft the spirit high. But long before
You dare to dream, you must accept the bond
That ties you fast to world's reality,
That when the mist of dreams awakened harsh
Condenses cold, the warmth within your heart
Will keep at bay the tears of dire regret.

Beyond

Yearning

A thought that saddens deep my yearning heart
Is knowing that tomorrow never brings
The resolution I anticipate,
As back that day recedes from now e'ermore.

But yet, if evermore the fate of man
Is charted fast upon a changeless course,
Then whence and wherefore comes this yearning hope
Whose failing saddens woefully my heart?

The Motion of the Universe

Consider now this orb which flies through space
Around the sun, just as its moon doth fly,
And even so do comets fly apace
In orbits of inordinate design.

Will any orb or any group of them,
In any part of all the universe,
Convert their spatial motion natural
To any but a motion orbital?

John Niemirovich

Of God and Man

As like unto the ruling architect,
By virtue of his multiplicity,
Has man invented and erected works
That spring profusely from his active mind.

By virtue of their multiplicity,
Am I, observer, overwhelmed by them—
The works of man's design before me spread—
That truly are the wonders of the world.

And how shall I, with mortal mind and eye,
Begin to tally all the works of God.

The Actor

Depicting life in dramas staged by man
The striving actor played his part so well
He soon forgot that life was surely not
A make believe, but model to the play.

As time went by and roles were few between,
He felt, the plays the thing and only thing,
That nothing else would ever do for him,
And so he pined away to nothingness.

Beyond

Extinction

Another species lately has appeared
Upon the burgeoning endangered list.
A list prepared by a superior
Who shares the crowded, shrinking world, not owns.
The torturous and painful upward path
That man has carved from sluggish ignorance
To lofty heights of facile competence
Enables him each different kind of life
To sort into its proper niche unique.
The knowledge gained is of awareness
But not of foresight—extinction to forestall.
Apprised as man now is, he feigns concern
And watches as each species calmly meets
Its premature, lamentable demise
Precipitated by the careless course
Of his events. And when the fragile world
No longer sings, to what will mankind listen?

Swift Time

Swift time, the enemy of restless youth
Who would accomplish more than time allows,
Becomes benevolent to fading age
Whose hours are filled with more than time allows.

John Niemirovich

Grief

The sad goodbye between dear parting friends
Though keenly felt with numbing drear effect,
Is prelude to the final parting when
The pall of all embracing grief descends.

Intellect

Though first impressions satisfy our yen
To quickly sort the problems near at hand,
Inquiry and analysis alone
Can lead to a conclusion just and fair.

To Be Or Not To Be

The fleeting question now and then appears,
Within the panorama of my mind,
If we exist or not? If not, I trow,
There nothing is that's worth considering.

Priority

I see a thousand things that must be done,
All racing through my mind, all clamoring
And all demanding its priority,
But only one at any time can win.

Beyond

Who Do We Think We Are?

Precipitously standing on the brink
Of vast eternity, I wonder why
We must endure the pain of grief imposed
Upon our lives by others such as we?

Departed Friend

He walked the Earth as you and I do now,
And when I search the gallery of my mind,
I see the phantom of his memory,
Though he has wafted to eternity.

When?

Do not concern yourself with your demise;
Live on and laugh or weep as chance dictates,
And while you dance and merry make with chance,
The specter fate will pick the time to go.

Supply and Demand

The price of staying alive has risen to heights
So rarified that resolution trembles
When looking down to see oft only gold
Can pamper honesty to persevere.

John Niemirovich

Truth

The art of lying permeates some minds
To such alarming extent there's hardly room,
Within its hallowed chambers, to admit
The barest semblance of veracity.

Here We Are

The surest sign a nation has arrived,
Has reached the peak of cultural assault,
Is that its soldiers die by lot assigned
And not defensive dire necessity.

And Then

Will Christ a ransom be for flesh of man,
To be again a man of flesh, though flesh
Has once belied its sacred trust in life,
Or will this renaissance be more than flesh?

Starry Sky

Although it's magnified through telescope,
The starry sky recedes beyond my sight
To distant vast, too vast to understand,
And I am struck with insignificance.

Beyond

Man and Fate

The spark was struck, the flame of thought enkindled.
In time forgot, emerging man, entranced,
Did stare into this fire as time sped by
Outpacing far the faltering gait of thought.
But now the rush of thought outpaces time
And either man or fate must step aside.

The Spirit of Spring

The chill of winter has no joy unless
The heart is by anticipation warmed.
The joy, unvoiced although profoundly felt,
Of looking forward to the coming spring,
Uplifts the spirit wan to travel on
To share again the mystery of life
With man and beast and all the growing plants.

Limit

Though we, who are composed of flesh and blood,
A form of energy and matter dense,
Are touched by substances mainly such as we,
Still some will strive to learn what lies beyond.

John Niemirovich

The Light of Day

Behold the sun, the furnace far in space,
Of nuclear design it radiates
The energy of life to planet Earth.
A flaming sphere whose fleeting rays of light
Excite all substances both near and far
And gives to them the color and the form
That strikes our sight with wonders infinite.

And Space

The universe of matter, energy,
And empty space is rightly so composed,
For otherwise there no container is
Where energy and matter may exist.

Birth

The birth of life unfolds another child
And life rejoices of this innocence
Which, frail, soon fades when other life it meets
Where competition dominates the cycle.

To W. S.

Now back I'll reach to times more sweet and gentle
When every promise passed between was sacred,
And any dream come true or rendered false
Was warmed with sunny smile or washed with tear.

Beyond

Fact and Fancy

In spite of all the ego man may muster
To bravely bruit his splendid worthiness
Or learned, pious dignity, it seems
That he created naught of what he is.

But will the day arrive when man can take
The creature bold and brash that now he is
And mold a being more in keeping with
The thing he thought he ought have ever been?

Death

This vacant, uncomplaining thing I see
Is filled with all the mystery of life,
Though life has fled beyond the veil of knowing
And left behind a mute and mocking puzzle.

Love

So frail a thing is love as felt between
The likes of you and me who only wait
For fate to guide us through our fleeting lives,
The wonder is that love would deign exist.

John Niemirovich

Relentless Adversity

Dejected, I stand and look at all the world
Yet not submissive to its challenges,
Its endless erosive adversity, but rather
As weary of its dull, unchanging dread.

The Child

The spirit soars to distant regions rare
And never tires of new discoveries,
Yet flesh is weak and must be tended soft
And guided as the trusting child it is.

Spring 1980

It's spring again, again our hemisphere
Has tilted to the long awaited sun
Whose rays oppose the chill of winter past
And stir the slumber deep of bated life.

Time

When I would feel the rushing pulse of time,
Its stern demanding beat inevitable
Reverberates concern within my breast,
But how ignore the drummer's cadent roll?

Beyond

Giants

The giants of yesterday, who loom so large
Within my wondering and searching mind,
Departed have yet still their memory
Is wrapt in awesome substance durable.

Entropy

I see the elemental force at work
Relentlessly reclaiming all the works
Which man has wrought. In quantum visible it nears
To test the faith that guides the fate of man.

The Guiding Force

The stars above are subject to the forces
Of gravity and fusion twain, which race
Through space and time, as Aesop's hare and
 tortoise,
Where flash of fusion pales to gravity.

Distraction

The soul, so closely interwoven with
The fleshy fabric of the body dross,
Forgets its higher purpose here on Earth
When human passions clamor round about.

John Niemirovich

Across the Ages

Between the ages of our lives apart
There stretches an expanse of time and space
That bids my mind return to time at hand
To marvel at your erstwhile presence here.

Beyond

Why weep, yet weep I do, for bells that toll
When men and women born of flesh depart
While deep inside I feel that all I see
Is not the end of all there is to see?

The Hand of Fate

Who guides my erring footsteps unerringly,
From place to place in fascination to see
The mysteries portrayed by wily fate
Which serve anticipation to intrigue?

The Power of Love

The power of love commands chaotic fate
To put aside the clamoring multitude
Of voiceless desires attending ego
That we may taste the selfless joy of life.

Beyond

Transit

How many souls, bedecked in finery of clay,
Have briefly stopped to touch this earth
Then shed their temporary accoutrement
To fly away to airy realms beyond?

To Love

To think of love and know that others, too,
Do think of loving you as you of others;
To search for love while others also search;
To know of love; yet doubt it's all in vain.

Moments

Alone with frantic and confused assessment
Of desperately hoping they've not been squandered,
The moments of my life relentlessly
Arouse me only to betake their swift adieu.

Bon Voyage

A child is cast upon the sea of life
To sink or swim to rocky hostile shore,
To make his way through troubled times and drear;
Perhaps ensnared by waiting undertow.

John Niemirovich

Fantasy?

I saw a gaping wound that spurted blood
Which drenched my dream until I screamed in fear;
At once the wound became a pair of lips
That sipped a glass of deeply colored wine.

The Uninvited Guest

In irritating, chiding syllables
Within the inner sanctum of my self,
In voiceless whisper, the voice of conscience hists,
An ever present, uninvited guest.

Exposure

The years that journey through eternity
Are infinite in scope of fluid events;
In contrast to this panorama vast,
Our time on Earth appears a snapshot mere.

Hate

The hate of flesh by flesh is strange to see
Unless that hate be disembodied soul
That is encumbered by unruly pride
And wears the mantle of man in churlish spite.

Beyond

A Crowd of One

The atoms numberless that spin about
Are massed into a finite store from which
The Earth conceives a teeming multitude
Of individuals unique in form.

A Glimpse

I saw you walking by and wondered why
The hurried wings of time and circumstance
So swiftly bore you out of view and left
A vanished image of confused desire.

To J. S.

If, when I've read your story to its end,
I see amid the turbulence of life,
The eddies you have stilled upon your page,
I'll marvel at your art and maybe weep.

The Unanswered Question

I heard your voices pleading soft to know
The why and wherefore of this life on earth:
The words were poignant, sweet the melody;
The sacred song of life across the ages.

John Niemirovich

War's Cemetery

In testimony mute and stark they lie,
The victims who became the prize of War,
While War in haughty deference
Awaits amused the offering next of man.

Sally

My disability has not inured
My heart and mind to fear and failure;
If you will look beyond infirmity,
You'll see my spirit struggling to achieve.

Moralist

Before you take it upon yourself to speak
Against the moral laxities you see
I'm sure you will concur wholeheartedly
Not every indiscretion's publicized.

The Mystery of Life

The mystery of life is always there,
Beyond the edge of busy consciousness,
And now and then will breach, with moment great,
To overwhelm distractedness with awe.

Beyond

A Rare View

I do not know why God has made this world
Or why amid its harsh realities
He placed occasional views of beauty
That gladden exquisitely our harried hearts.

Born of Yesterday

How many thoughtful minds have attempted
To trace the course that future generations
Will travel through the untold years to come;
How many of us know that here we are?

My Love Beyond

I know I love, yet know not what love is.
I see the forms I love, but soon those forms
Evaporate unto a realm beyond
And there in mystery resides my love.

The Mystic's Quest

It all begins with you, the entity.
Be happy with the creature born to you,
Stray not too far in quest of greater glory;
Your quest may lead your essence to decay.

John Niemirovich

The Hypocrite

I loathe the weaknesses I see in others
And will not understand why it is they
Would willingly demean themselves with that
Which in myself I deem as meet and right.

The Quiet Path

The grass-lined path was worn through trees grown
    dense
Whose trunks were arched into a passageway
Wherein I sensed a soothing innocence,
As nature's strife were caught in harmless play.

In truth I felt as though I were intruding
When steeped within its permeating balm,
And felt a pang within my breast of brooding
That life as lived could never be as calm.

Faded Dream

He feels his life has gone. It went the way
Of many setting suns and summers fair,
It was expended on a dream that fades;
No matter now, for nothing else sufficed.

Beyond

The Silent Hills of Leni-Lenape

How many silver moons ago, that shone
In softened splendor o'er the Delaware,
Since last these hills, in soughing verdant grown,
Resounded laughter Leni-Lenape fair?

The lodges long have since been struck and moved
To unseen sites beyond the worldly sun
Where only spirits dwell, by Fate reproved,
To tell their tales of Nations proud undone.

Encroaching doom was borne upon the dreams
That blew the mast through calm and stormy sea
With laden manifest of future schemes
To crash upon the shores of Leni-Lenape.

With quiet overture the natives met
The travelers come across the water wide
To see, amid their wonder and regret,
This mystery that came upon the tide.

In Nature's trusted bond they lived and thrived
No match for threats designed by thoughts complex
That brushed aside their every ploy contrived,
With brash impunity their souls to vex.

The overwhelming forces onward massed
Engulfing all the land from coast to coast
Until the time when sovereignty was passed
To searching immigrant from native host.

The tribe of Leni-Lenape has scattered far
To distant hills and streams there steps have wended;
Their lives are guided by another star.
Another chapter thus of man has ended.

John Niemirovich

The Farmer

The farmer toils beneath the blazing sun
Disdaining not to furrow through the dust
That others, far beyond his caring toils,
May sup the labored bounty of his hands.

Bittersweet

Within the labyrinth of memory
Reside remembrances of long ago,
Encountered first in childhood's adventure,
That now and then emerge with poignant joy.

The Other Person

However clinical the observation,
Within the object of perusal
There lives a sentient being assailed
By all concerns and fears besieging life.

Vessels

Waste not your anger on the thing you see
But rather look within the vessel clay,
Whose outward features harmlessly were fashioned,
And seek its hidden motivations there.

Beyond

Faith

The longer that I live the more I see
That which I call myself is not myself;
I see a finite set of actions strict
To which responds my faith, the only me.

Violent Crimes

The suicide who kills that he may reap
A pity posthumous unto himself
A murder violent commits and is
Below the one who kills to ease his pain.

Perspective

I wonder, is the universal plan
Sequential or extemporaneous.
Does every event proceed from prior event,
Or is the guiding force a timeless flux?

Apart From God

Though God created man, man cannot say
That he is God though he be good as gold:
He must be man though good or bad he be;
He must but work within the will of God.

John Niemirovich

The Masque

The saddening imperfections myriad
That permeate this costume flesh we wear—
Our entree to the masque of consciousness—
Obscure our search for inner excellence.

Ripples

I see myself a searching, sentient speck,
A mote upon the cosmos mystery,
Within a spectacle seemingly so obvious
Until I try to understand its essence;
At once its fragile image disappears
As though it were imposed upon the smooth
And speckled surface of a sylvan pool
Whose mystic repose is rippled by my thoughts.
Anon returns the flawless surface to reflect
Again the tantalizing view of life
So near to mind yet ever far beyond.

Beyond

Eternity

I see your face and momentarily
Illusion paints a picture of eternity
Whose splendid image fills my consciousness;
But as I gaze upon this fantasy
Reality dissolves its airy charm
And leaves behind the sober truth
That we are two whose tenancy is short,
Is leased sequentially to others as we.
Yet through it all persistently appears
A lingering vague hint of eternity.

Imperfect

I am convinced, in spite of doubts galore,
The world that God created is beautiful
And so too are the people in it, I swear;
It is their willful spirits are awry.

Decisions

Careening through the rigid do's and don'ts
Engendered by fallacious renderings,
I hurl through life now timid, anon bold,
And ever hope my journey safely ends.

John Niemirovich

A Fond Farewell

Once again the warmth of summer quickly flees
To dream and dally in another clime
While autumn's spectrum signals winter's chill
And icy days to fill the time between.

A Puzzle of Life

I wonder why the incidence of man
So awed my dawning awareness of life
When, after much of troubled morality,
I find that he exactly is myself?

Knowledge

The knowledge shared by those contemporary
Though awesome in its rigid, strict demands
Is but a frozen snapshot of yesterday
That time will meld into a common truth.

The Indian's Burial

Upon the windswept Andes near the sky
They laid her body frail within a grave
That barely scratched the titan mountaintop.
Upon her thin and careworn, frozen face,
Where once her spirit shone, a tiny grin
Which emphasized the endless mystery.

Beyond

Mortals

Yea, they were beings mortals cast adrift
To soar in fear upon the planet Earth
Through the wide expanse of starry dust
Without the wherewithal to battle demons.

Technology

A long and hazy look into the past
Of man and of myself detects a view
Of Earth and growing things that grew with man,
And man was fast within this entity.
By fate's design and man's tenacity
This ancient entity evolved in twain
As instinct, and a searching intellect
Which saw itself and fashioned its release.
In hesitant and faltering efforts uprose
The challenged spirit of man till he
Emerged above the teeming course of life;
The wonder of the sights complex he saw
Astonished so his germinating mind
He quite forgot, as careless time sped by,
The common roots he shared with other forms.
That long forgotten bond does still exist,
Extinct alone within the mind of man
As man and earth continue in a growth
That must be tempered with that bond relearned.

John Niemirovich

Odyssey

The dangers of the unknown were less
To be concerned about than those at home,
A myriad of devastating ills,
Replete with hunger pangs to prod their fears;
Depart they must at once to any fate.
But how escape the stifling, cramped confines
That quenched their lives though not their burning dreams?
At once the open sea with freedom's smile
Did lure and beckon them to test their mettle.
In mute anticipation, huddled close
In wretched quarters, bravely did they dare
To leap the killing bonds of slavery.
Adrift for grueling hours upon the sea,
The refugees were nigh upon the main
When churning, pounding waters rose to beat
The overburdened craft of rotted planks.
The spilling waves were ruthless in their might
As in their brute embrace the craft capsized
To empty all into the fatal fray.
The weakened swimmers burst their lungs in vain
As roaring waters choked their burning dreams;
The human flotsam washed upon the shore,
A ghastly reminder of freedom's worth.
To those who stood before the broken dreams
And mused upon the vagaries of fate,
Who turns the pages of the book of life,
No easy answer came to calm their doubts,
Though some were sure to know within their hearts
The sea gives life to all upon this earth
By virtue of its awesome vital force,
But woe to those who slip upon its waves.

Beyond

The Sounds of Love

How strange it is that we appear to be
So common in our mask of flesh and blood,
Yet from this locus of mortality
There issues forth the sweetest sounds of love.

A Special Face

The faces passing by are known to me
And framed within the gallery of life;
Your image, known to me, confuses me
With special thoughts exposed in softer light.

Again

The world will spin a painful turn or two
While I forget to dream of foolish love
And wonder why I was unwise again,
Until I'm foolishly in love again.

Silence

Contained within the mirthless labyrinth
Of this my lonely world, I heard a voice,
Your voice, demanding sweetly to be heard;
But now you've gone, the silent days are sad.

John Niemirovich

Compassion

Old Galileo bowed before the men
Whose laws have proven less than those required.
The men are gone; their judgment lingers on:
But Galileo's laws have theirs outpaced.

A Vain Pursuit

The vanity of conquering the world
Has lured a multitude to emptiness.
Indeed, how conquer the unconquerable?
Instead, seek ye the essence of the world.

From Dust to Dust

From gathered dust the stars are formed
Which radiate the energy of life
By which we wend our perilous journey
Until the darkened day we turn to dust.

The Chosen Few

Who casts the fatal lot to draw the names
From nations' registers to send to war,
Amid hurrahs and martial music brazen,
Those faithful few to face the fears of war?

Beyond

The Unique Commonality

The teeming population of the world
Is numbered in the billions, burgeoning
This lonely orb with endless diversity,
Yet there is only one of each of us.

Earthly Pleasures

As thin as air, my pleasures follow me:
In music's melody engulfing me,
Or voices sweet that sue for love's demands;
But where to go for substance durable?

Generations

The time of man on earth is short and swift;
It flies from age to age in careless haste
Compounding individual resolve
Which blends into the common lore of life.

The Spirit of Man

The laws of nature naught demand from life
But strict compliance for continuance.
It is the remnant of man's soul primeval,
His spirit, strives to kindle the spark of love.

John Niemirovich

Smiles

A beautiful and winning smile of joy
Is brighter than the brightest flower that blooms;
Its delicate, endearing radiance
Distills sheer happiness from heavy hearts.

Resolution

If I were free to choose, I'd rather souls
Of self-determination, shunning those
Whose resolution flees like autumn's leaves
Before the slightest, whispered, vagrant breeze.

Christmas

The Christmas season fills our lives with joy
In glad anticipation of a love
That freely spreads throughout from heart to heart,
But too intense for earthly residence.

Pearl Harbor

The memory dims of still another battle
That killed and maimed the memory of peace.
The God of War was pleased that fatal day
To see another lapse of memory.

Beyond

My Love

My perfect love, the image unattached
Unceasingly demands I search in quest
Of one whose kindred spirit may unleash
The slavish bonds of earth's hostility.

Today Is Not Forever

Today is not forever, waste it not,
Its moments rare are won by stern resolve.
Not all tomorrow's days shall dawn for thee,
Take care today's demands are fully met.

A Dream Is Love

A dream is love that will not let me be.
In vain its charms I banish from my heart;
It seeks and beckons me unto its arms,
But when I would respond it will not stay.

John Niemirovich

Events

The time of all our lives is paralleled
By time of all the universe, which flows
In endless stream beyond our moment brief
And is accented by a series of events,
Events that swiftly pass beyond our reach
Although were some we would have thought to keep.

In memory alone do they exist,
That seemed so large and real a while ago.
So large and real they were before our eyes,
We thought for sure they must exist in dream.
We little thought how true that fleeting insight
As presently we sit and scan the dream.

It seems events occur apart from us,
That we are both observer and event.

Dame Nature

Dame Nature's plan to populate the world
Is mandatory in participation.
Demanding first compliance then, perhaps,
If so it pleases, allowing constancy.

Beyond

The First Kiss

Her lovely offered lips were soft and cool
Not warm and scented as are roses pink
That blush in bloom beneath the loving sun,
But soft with promise chaste of warmer days.

My Faith

A mortal man am I whose doubts and fears
Will sometimes a mockery make of faith
But through it all I fervently do pray
That I be thankful faith endured assault.

The Currency of Love

We love each other as our hearts desire
And count our love as currency unmatched,
But in this world our currency's unhonored;
Hence mortgage we our love to pay the world.

Foolish Dreams

There's nothing in this harsh and heartless world,
Whose poisoned sting is balmed by soothing dreams,
More devastates our equanimity
Than foolish dreams that e'er evade our grasp.

John Niemirovich

After the Promise

The haste demanded of love, which panics
In jealous rage all others to forestall,
Creates a whirlwind filled with promises
That soon descend upon the hapless pair.

Love's Delay

Love's tedious delay of consummation desired
By patient, understanding suitors keen,
Who must endure the world's hostility,
At times does strain its credibility.

Dark Eyes

My love has eyes as dark as darkest night,
In vain I look to see my heart's delight;
But when she deigns to open wide her eyes
This weary world becomes a paradise.

Beyond

The Stuff of Love

Most unsubstantial is the stuff of love
Which quickly disappears to nothingness.
Where once the heart cavorted high above
It soon descends to hell in bitterness.
Where are the burning sighs that sear the heart
In glad, unbearable anticipation sweet;
The joy of ended weary hours apart
That torture with illusions of conceit;
The honeyed vows of love's devotion dear,
The song the heart conceals of paradise;
The courage fierce that turns aside all fear,
The longing looks from love's enticing eyes;
Where are these dreams that lovers new accrue
When once that love undying proves untrue?

Destinies

I wonder whether' all events exist
Within a universe of timelessness
And are sequentially exposed to us
According to determined destinies?

Confused Desire

We search the world our loneliness to ease
For someone different from all the others
Yet when we find that someone different
We wish that someone were as like as all.

John Niemirovich

The Ancient Earth

We move upon the Earth forgetting that
Our ties to it inseparable are.
A patient Earth shrugs off our unconcern.
It scars received by us will disappear
Enfolded deep within its curling crust
Through patient aeons eclipsing frantic man
And possibly man's destiny renounced.

Babel

The teeming multitudes of devotees,
In mindless strife determined to outdo,
Deplete creative energies of man
For common goals confused by selfishness.

Deceit

Deceit is nothing more than charming mien
Which falsely pictures to unpracticed eyes
The sum of all the motives deep within
Which surface eventually themselves revealing.

Beyond

Redemption

I held an apple, a seedling of that fruit
Whose bitter lore did banish man from Eden,
But sweetened by the husbandry of man,
It seemed a promise of redemption's value.

Selfish Songs

Not all the songs of freedom ringing clear,
That hail the unsuspecting standing by,
Are sung to praise democracy's concern,
But oft are plaints of childish selfishness.

Alone at Last

Each mortal being stands alone in life
And must in time his destiny accept
Which strikes an awesome chord within his heart
Of sad departure from the breast of life.

Scribbling

In spite of fervent resolutions of mine
To scribble never more another line
To unrequited love, I've racked my brain
For passionate words of limbo's lonely pain.

John Niemirovich

The Hate of Love

Sweet love is fragile as a petal soft
And wilts before the mindless meddlesome mob
When bold desire, to balm its aching heart,
Must plead its case in strident terms of hate.

Love's Venture

I asked for everything, though not with words,
But touched the heart of you with heart of mine
Convinced that you could never fail to see
This sweetness must be lover's proof of trust;
But now I know that lover is a fool
Who thinks his tender love will never harm
The object of his yearning heart's desire.
To touch the beating heart of someone loved
And leave it still unscathed as once it was
Is far beyond our mortal competence;
Indeed, how can a perfect bond endear,
For who has ever loved without a tear?

Prologue

The dream is prologue to accomplishment,
It soothes away the many fretful hours
Which plague the enterprising acts of those
Who must by laws complex attempt the prize.

Beyond

Hidden Hate

The lurking hate that lies within our minds
So deeply hidden its barbs are never felt
Or its inception blurred remembered not
Oft strikes with senseless vengeance those we love.

Surprize

The fates, who mete our destinies unknown,
Are privy to the unexpected turns
That rudely greet our shocked realities
When glib delusion promised otherwise.

An Unanswered Question

I called upon the powers to reveal
The essence of the beings such as I
Who flood the world with endless replicas
And saw a ghostly figure mutely stern.

My Love

What if my love is not enough for you,
If all the fancies that my ego deems
Of worth commensurate your beauty rare,
Are merely efforts vain that please your whim?

John Niemirovich

Swirling Doubts

In doubtful apprehensions travel we
The twisting turns that ever harry us
Who are but handfuls of encumbered dust
Immersed within a world of swirling dreams.

There

I now can see that there is nothing there,
No future hope nor pleasant memories,
There but remains the inner pangs of love
That must be soothed soft by patient time.

The Realm of Time

If here and now, our mortal time to be aware,
Is all there is to time and its events
Then time can have no other place to pass
And threads infinity through needle's eye.

Beyond

The Song of Time

Tell time to stop its merry chimes
Which ring melodious
For those who have no caring rhymes,
While those more studious
Can only hear
The sound of fear.

But time will pass the while away
With all events arranged
To challenge minds into the fray
Till every brain's deranged
And spiritless will say
That fate and time hold sway.

Social Identity

I see beyond the social image bright
You wear upon your face and in your aura
Until I feel the basic form of life,
Then marvel more its tenuous veneer.

A Lover's Dilemma

I will attenuate my fierce desire,
The less your sweetness to intimidate,
If you'll reciprocate and not accuse
My ego of a stuffy, vain conceit.

John Niemirovich

Iris

The rainbow's many colors dazzling bright
Are apt comparison to all the moods
That shine across your lovely, winning face
From innocence to bold, seductive dare.

Remembered Pollywogs of Childhood

I came across a teeming pool of life,
A basin formed of mud and filled with rain,
The lavish gift of spring to celebrate
The reemergence of another year.

Adios

No longer filled with rushing, harsh events
Demanding all my nervous energy,
Which I expend for grateful loss of pique,
This weary day will soon be lost to time
To take its place within the misty past
Which lives alone in doubtful memory.

Spatial Exploration

Say, how explore the starry universe,
A vast arena spatial scattered through
With tiny specs of fleeting permanence
So far apart the speed of light seems slow?

Beyond

The Human Condition or Prelude to Faith

Condition human, how to deal with it?
The passing centuries abound with it
In myriad of individuals
Unique in being though in essence not
Which threads through each and every one of us.
The essence with its immortality
Intimidating our mortality
Anon uplifting it with promised joy:
But through it all remains in doubt and fear
The mortal entity whose being clay
Immersed in searching meditation deep
Must weather all alone the stormy thoughts
Of knowing life and death are common woes
That rush to grasp our individual concern.

Tears

Weep, weep, O weep no more for life's a game,
A game of dreams to while away the hours
As harsh reality demands its due,
And only God has love enough to weep.

Tomorrow

The day is set aside when fate decrees
Tomorrow's morn will never dawn for me,
But in my dreamy consciousness I see
To travel on I must expect that dawn.

John Niemirovich

St. Patrick

The favored youth was captured from his home
And lived awhile in Eire's wilderness.
He fled his captives to escape his bond
But never broke the bond of Ireland.

Caprice

I could attribute your capriciousness
To inexperience in love's allure
But dread the thought of wounded vanity
And its destructive, fiery response.

Hopes and Dreams

A world in which there are no hopes or dreams
To nurture and sustain the soul of man,
Who ever strives for goals beyond his reach,
Becomes a world of charnel house despair.

The Vibrancy of Spring

The trees are stark across the countryside,
The chill of winter is in the air,
But unmistakably there hovers near
The vibrancy of spring's awakening.

Beyond

The Chemistry of Life

The generations pour into the world,
A vial of semen and a vial of cells
By master chemist mixed to potency
That streams throughout the crowded biosphere.

The Game of Life

The game we play is ruled by laws complex
But under all the glitter lies the truth,
The sum of all you do is woman hight,
A woman hight are you and I a man.

Social Involvement

Instinctively involved with those around
We live our lives in sympathetic trust
Until the mystic bond is torn apart;
At once we question moral paucity.

John Niemirovich

Adam's Child Unbound

A roaring, shuddering and wondrous leap
Through glowing clouds of billowing exhaust
Takes man into the endless realm of space.
A daring child of God he now becomes
To hurl in future days through outer space,
Among the flaming stars catapulted.
In imitation of the grand design,
He charts his course in orbit bound by him
And rides with universal gravity.
Too long he tarried fettered to the earth
And ever yearned to break the heavy bond
While soared his mind to heights ethereal.
From ages past of earthbound reverie
The journey now begins to track the paths
That erst were traveled only in his mind.

The Goal of Man

The shuttlecraft returned to waiting earth
And while in proud and grand descent, I heard,
It seemed, the declaration, "Man am I.
I've soared awhile in distant regions rare.
Perhaps one day the galaxy I'll tour
In search of knowledge of the universe
Whose answers will enlarge my mortal view
Of all the ages past and those to come."

Beyond

Flux

Seek not for permanence, for none there is,
But learn acceptance of inconstant flux.
For flux there is that flows eternally
Or else a frozen universe there is.

My Changing Love

My changing love has never been accused
Of being constant in her vows of love,
But changes she her mind from vow to vow
Again, again, again, and yet again.

Guess Who Again?

My feckless love has never been accused
Of being resolute when love denies,
But keeps returning with foolish hope
Again, again, again, and yet again.

The Image of Man

The outward image shown to us of man
Is that delineating his descent
Through ages of sophisticated lore
Veneering inner churnings of his mind.

John Niemirovich

The Weary Sins of Man

As he embraces willingly their charms,
The weary sins of man pervade his realm
In never ending popularity
Though he is sated of their jaded fame.

A Remembered Idyllic Impression

The chirping insects deep in matted grass,
The singing birds on slender, bending twigs,
The croaking frog in murky, stagnant pool,
The heat of summer's balm embracing me
Beneath a sky of blue with fleecy clouds
That lazily are swept along the breeze,
While radiant the flowers blooming soft.

Budding Spring

The bitter blasts of winter past are gone,
Their icy cold assaults have all succumbed
Before the hesitant debut of spring
In budding green and lacey finery
That manifest the tender growth contained
Within the hoary crust of yesteryear.

Beyond

Us

The world with all the things that are within
Was built in grand, complex design by One
Who then the spirit Life infused through all
Whose incremental breath is each of us.

O Love

O love, say whence thy softness emanates
Ameliorating harsh realities;
Not here on Earth thy selfless trek begins,
For man responds to love, creates it not.

Why I?

The question oft arises in my mind
Of what I am and why I do exist
But never have the endless doubts been matched
With other than a nimbus flash of faith.

To Potter's Field

In spite of all the many faults of man,
And undeniable proof of nature's law
That all who live must wait the chill of death,
It's sad to see that some must die unloved.

John Niemirovich

The Tyranny of Love

The tyranny of love in its demands
Runs wildly through our hearts instilling fear
And wilts resolve through fiercely, flashing eyes
Until we speak with words of sweet concern.

The Guiding Force of Man

Mankind is born in droves across the earth
His brief tenure consumed by daily bouts
To eke his meager existence drear.
Whence those ideas to direct his fate?

The Seeds of Love

The seeds of love are scattered far and wide
To settle in the heart and mind of us
To grow or die upon the will of us
For only we can nurture love to grow.

Beyond

Dominance

Dame Nature, through a lavish gift of time,
Evolved reactions chemical, complex
Into instinctive traits to all her charge,
Which some there are would sweep away.

The Creator

Whatever you decide to call the force
Which built the universe in grand design,
It functions still with undiminished verve,
As witness all the stars and endless doubts.

Euthanasia

To kill in mercy is oft cruel deceit
That's practiced the observer to relieve
Of painful and unpleasant happenings.
Were more humane to suffer loved one's pain.

John Niemirovich

My Dreams

My dreams are dreams fantastic, born unique
Within my fevered brain, apart from all.
My dreams are wild and would destroy me quite.
My dreams are mad and hard to bear, O Lord!

May

The merry month of May has once again
Her secret bower enfolded lavishly
With growing grass and leaf on naked limb,
The prying eyes of all to turn aside.

The Death of Love

I loved not you but loved I love sweet love
That sugars sweet the bitter fare of life.
Forget your vain conceits and hateful spite;
I loved not you, but weep for love's demise.

Beyond

The Time Is Now

We see events occur sequentially
And reckon them the beat of time.
Its rhythm beats across the ages vast
With ages yet untold to pass before
Yet never greater in its scope than now,
This moment now is all there is to time.
It beats a rhythm far beyond our ken
But not beyond our mortal consciousness.
How as a line infinitesimal it sweeps
Across e'er shadowy limbo manifold
Repository holding all events.
The moving line is now and as it moves
It pushes back the dark of future time
Illuminating now to mind of man
And leaves its memory as on it moves.
Events occurring far beyond our sun
Are printed upon the page of speeding light
Which travels locked within the grasp of time
Until it bursts upon our distant sense.
Until we know of them they travel on
Through distant space in future time from us
Though to themselves the time they see is now
And we to them exist in future time.
A moment brief we know of them which pass
Unto the ages past, their time to us is past,
Though others wait in future time for them.

John Niemirovich

The Ruthless World

The world will not away, will not be gone,
Its cares and woes persist upon my view;
It delegates its challenges apace;
It tarries not when down at last I fall.

Two Strangers We

It is correct we knew each other not,
If my presumption needs apology
A dream is not a memory of love,
It is a promise of tomorrow's love.

D Day

The thunder shook the sand upon the beach
That drank the blood of bodies mutilated
While bloated comrades bobbed in silent waves
As Mars and man portrayed a grisly scene.

Function

The body we posses is fancy free
And functions purely to survive its time
Within the strict regime of this its world
While we in airy realms do ever pose.

Beyond

Friendship

The need for friendship lies within the mind
In depths beneath the surface all may see
To prop the sagging spirit, but its need
Must ripple not the placid surface sheen.

Tomorrow's Child

A thousand years will swiftly tell their time
While myriads of genes are rearranged
To form an individual unique.
I wonder what that person's name will be?

The Clock of Life

The clock of life is wound and running down
And we are rushing to and fro because
Allowing us but one response per beat
The moments tick away in jealous haste.

Strung Events

Is time the limitation of response
That forms a chain whose links are strung events
Each added in a stringent serial
The first event our birth the last our death?

John Niemirovich

Crackpot

The pot is tossed about with no regard
To damage it sustains each time it's chucked,
For after all it was not meant to last;
Who cares about another pot that's cracked!

Doubt

We live within surroundings dangerous,
We're fraught with doubt of what tomorrow brings.
The system functions now but will it fail?
In doubt we live within our bodies frail.

Antagonist

Created by benevolence, our form,
Where shines a force of love that overwhelms,
Is oft besieged and conquered by a force
Which ploys deception through our innocence.

Spirits

The warm impressions hovering about
This hallowed, happy place is essence rare
Of all your joyous laughter and your wit
When once in days of yore you traveled here.

Beyond

The Silly Goose

O, woe to me,
Alas, alack
I lack the knack
Myself to see.
Yet truth to be I disagree
With those who say
My merry way
Is fraught with stuff
Enough, enough
To help me see
The worst of me.

Dilemma

The thoughtless word that passed between us twain
Enraged my unsuspecting heart which vowed
To banish from my mind all thoughts of you,
Yet still it yearns to keep you warm within.

Tyrant

The tyrant strode into the light of day
Where for a time he held his sway;
He stretched his arm to grab a distant star,
But tripped instead and fell the other way.

John Niemirovich

Recompense

In pessimistic wail do some bemoan
Their narrow path on earth by habit worn
Then turn their eyes above for recompense;
They vow a better path, but not indeed.

Tomorrow's Time

Tomorrow's time is but a day away,
Beyond eternity is yesterday's;
It passed this way in manifold events
Of swirling matter stirred by energy.

Take Care

You have a conscience formed through God's design
And placed within the sum of what you are
But if you turn an ear that's deaf to it
A sterner voice will speak its ghostly charge.

Adieu Ingrid

We all must vanish from this earthly life
And trade our harried forms, consumed by time,
For tenuous continuance within
The memories of those who vanish too.

Beyond

The Garden of Life

A lovely flower blooms then withers and dies;
It's then replaced by other lovely flowers
That bloom then wither and die and on and on.
I wonder who has all this time and talent?

The Dream

What kind of dream is life, so near at hand,
Its pain and joy engrossing consciousness,
While underneath a constant fruitless search
For revelation of its mystery?

A Girl

I saw a girl in conversation bound
With family and friends gathered round.
She stood apart and seemed unsure of fate
As though her presence she must meditate.
She hesitated her place on earth to claim
Yet faced conventions strict their force to tame
That she her force of life could share
In personal desire and worldly care.

John Niemirovich

Complacency

There is no need for intervention from
The power lying beyond some daily lives
To punish or approve their acts or thoughts
For all of good or bad is one with them.

A Conflict Unresolved, Perhaps

The theory of evolution states
The individual is expendable;
The soul of man, which is the will of God,
As far as it is pure, might this deny.

A Window Through the Clouds

The sky was dark with rising, swirling clouds
That danced between the setting sun and me.
They played in prankish merriment
While far below their gloomy, pulsing light
The season autumn enticed the setting sun
To gleam through them as mellow, antique green.

Our Distant Love

Within our spirit lies a distant love
Remotely touching now and then our hearts,
With joy entrancing sweet our reverie,
But shies from flesh and blood capriciously.

Beyond

Harassment

Reverting to the state of wariness
To fend the many threats conceived by hate
Depletes the energy of life and love
That would and should be spent constructively.

Contrast

The vigorous and growing days of youth
Develop character sustaining traits
That clear the thorny paths of fame and fortune
Which time contrasts with trembling, feeble age.

Spirit-life

The flesh we bear in life was born of earth.
We are the children of a fertile Dame
Whose dust contains the elements of flesh
Infused with Spirit-Life, the gift of God.

My Earthly Life

When I would grasp my life within my hands
To hold it close and gaze upon its fate
It flies beyond my reach with spectral haste
Reminding me it's written on the wind.

John Niemirovich

Commonweal

My rapt concern for approbation's vote
Diminishes with every passing year
Yet still persists to my astonishment
As though the stretching thread will never snap.

Revelation

Events of long ago return to mind
With understated, devastating thrust,
A gentle reprise of realizations harsh
Endured by others through our unconcern.

Beauty

Into this world came beauty to amaze
The senses and the hearts of mortal folk.
It came that we might marvel its allure,
But question not, nor long posses its charm.

Beyond

A Mortal Question

Why weep for thee who live and breathe as I,
Who may in destiny's complexity
Outlive my mortal presumptive whim?

I weep for thee and thy mortality,
I weep for separation yet to come,
I weep for thee, my friend, dost thou for me?

Madness Accepted

Designing hellish schemes with silent hate,
Insanity enjoys its rampant course
Throughout the unsuspecting multitude,
Infecting it with madness in disguise
Which it accepts without a murmured word,
Too tame to question popular response.

John Niemirovich

The Sight of Mortality

The centuries of myriad events
Majestically evolve on awesome scale
Which we, whose lives are briefly lived in haste,
Can only see within our probing minds.

In Search of Me

If I could be the person I would be
I should control the very atoms wee
That ever spin within the heart of me,
But what I am is endless mystery.

Adam Again

A child is mortal man of Mother Earth
Whose atoms formed his being tenuous;
Through eons patiently she wrought the puzzle
She coiled genetically within his thighs;
This puzzle, man, through perseverance brash,
Unraveled has and laid before his impish eyes.
Will Adam's ancient sin be infantile
Compared to knowledge gained by modern man?

Beyond

Resignation

The moments lost in bitter denunciation
Of fates denial of things that might have been
Are quickly hushed in retrospect's reproof
That they, indeed, were never meant to be.

The Sum

The sum of what I am
Resides
Beyond my view
Though ever probes my searching mind.
The images
Of what I think I am
Subtract
Now add
To rearrange the sum.

Poet

A child, in awe of all I see and know,
Withdrawn from all the world in expectation,
I ply the meter of my pleading verse
That gently probes the world for understanding.

John Niemirovich

Our Share of Time

Though time to each of us is but a blur
That seldom has the time to spend with us,
As on it dashes through eternity,
It gives to each of us our share of it.

Gentle Spirits

Where are the gentle spirits once did cross,
In misty ages past, my troubled path
Which down I walked in youth with eyes that saw
Too many things my heart could bear at once?

The Seeds of Thought

The fecund seeds of thought within my mind
Are ever seeking fertile ground to thrive,
In pell-mell haste my checks they quite ignore.
Who tossed those restless seeds within my mind?

The Course of Life

The safest course of life undoubtedly
Is that which steers a careful, chosen course
Between the rocks within the channel deep
Opposed to one which blindly picks a point.

Beyond

The Universe and Man

How far the farthest blazing stars unseen
Whose light may greet our expectation
When long to scattered dust they have returned?
Within the solitude of contemplation,
The thought of absolute immensity
Amazes me with boundless wondering,
But then another thought amazes more:
The wide expanse of universal scope,
The swift and endless course of passing time
Are blotted out of mind in swiftest haste
When frailest humankind intrudes my view.

Of Love

A thousand years will pass—a million—more—
And you and I and all and everything
Will blend within the lasting absolute
That once did pulse with love and hope and dreams.

The endless nothingness that looms before
Bestirs a puzzling question deep within,
If all we are so surely disappears
Why bother we to love and hope and dream?

John Niemirovich

Alone Almost

I see the children dancing quietly;
They wear a feigned and doubtful unconcern;
They dance to soothing music sweetly played
By merrymakers steeled to doubts and fears.

Around the floor they whirl on feet so light
They seem suspended in a dream, a dream
One dreams in fretful tossing somnolence
The harsh realities of life to flee.

Their hearts would dance away their fretting cares,
But in their minds resides the sober truth
Of endless, tenuous mortality
In which we're all enmeshed till doom us part.

The tantalizing truth of life's demands
Pervades their dance with now a merry note
And now a somber one that halts their step.
Perplexed they carry on their aimless waltz.

This vision from my view recedes afar
And as the dancers are reduced in size
My eyes detect a glowing luminance
Embracing unawares the dancing troop.

Beyond

The Search

A perfect love is love without desire,
Without desire because of consummation;
But in the spirit lies a restless urge
To search for something more than consummation:
It drives the spirit to a ceaseless search,
It keeps alive the need for something more;
The search becomes the driving force of life,
And love is seen as death of love's desire.

Fate

If fate controls our lives, as some have said,
Then every step we walk and breath we breathe
Apportioned is by ghostly force unseen
And naught we do is ours, nor thought nor deed.

Absent Heart

There will be others with your charm and grace,
Those born of generations following,
For I can see no end of friendly folk;
But though they work their charm on kindred hearts,
Which beat together in their wonderments
Of youthful revelations newly found,
They cannot move to joy this lonely breast.

John Niemirovich

The Face of Death

The face of death, though ever hovering near
Within the darkened chambers of my mind,
Unnerves me less than once it did until
It takes the form of those I cherish most.

What If?

If all the reasons for my confidence
Which sees me through all confrontations mad
With self-sustaining, saving, moral support
Should prove to be illusion sheer—alas!

The Will of God

We bend our wills to those we love of flesh.
It galls us not the least but comforts us.
How easy then a loving God obey;
Prefer: he sternly bade us bend our wills?

The Abyss

Will any soul abiding in body smug,
With no regard for rights of other folk,
Successfully attain the world beyond,
Or will it fall into the chasm between?

Beyond

A Stronger Force

The world perceived in youth with faithful eyes
Which saw a life of splendor under skies
That whether blue or gray yet ever smiled,
Becomes in age a pall of faithless lies.

Beneath this pall the failing spirit hides
While all around glib perfidy abides
As ever on it waxes in its strength
And halting, struggling decency derides.

But deeper yet than spirit cognizant
Abides a stronger force full militant
To prod anew this failing entity
To muster resolution adamant.

Facade

I see the smile you wear upon your face,
Your readiness to please gratuitously
With real concern for others' happiness;
I know the searing pain that burns within.

John Niemirovich

The Dirge of Death

If Death would stride the earth in silence wrapt
To reap his harvest sown of mortal flaw,
Intelligence could catalogue his deeds
With equal force among Dame Nature's laws.
In mystic bond, howe'er, within ourselves,
Emotion plies, an outward reaching force
That ever seeks to melt the rules of reason
With scalding tears of lamentation's wail.
Thus Death becomes a specter wrapt in fear
When we the dirge within our hearts do hear.

March is Here and April Near

Awake! for spring is near; forget your dreams,
Deep sleeping seeds beneath the frozen earth;
The crystal snow is sprung to mirthful streams,
The sun returns to speed your vernal birth.

Greetings

My greetings come to you while I'm away,
A part of us and all our joy are they.
They come from deep within my beating heart
To speak of constant love though we're apart.
I send them winging on their way, my sweet,
Till once again in time and place we meet.

Beyond

To Do

I tried to squeeze into this hurried day
The many things I thought it best to do,
To hold my own with pride before the fray,
But really did but what I had to do.

Naked Destiny

When all the music they would hear is played,
When all the candy, cars, and stereos,
When all the goodies man conceives is theirs,
Will they be pleased with naked destiny?

Time's Capacity

Compared to time, in its eternity,
Our life is short; its length is like
The briefest spark that quickly glows and dies.
Within this span of time, into our lives
Events are pressed in density compact
Which makes us marvel times capacity
And doubt at times that time is ever sated.

John Niemirovich

Continuity

Consider the time of now, how close it seems,
How clear we see the view of this our world.
This view is seen and felt and analyzed,
Its wonders lavishly expressed with skill.
By a veneer of continuity,
These wonders span the past and woven are
Of ever changing gossamer to clothe
A dreamy wisp of fleeting, fleshy stuff.

My Mind

What madness, madness flames within my mind?
My what? My mind? Is that the endless source
Of searing pain that rages back and forth
To check my every view upon the world?

If that it is then I and it exist
As entities apart, at war always,
For I can never hope to live at peace
With willful, prodding thoughts, if not my own.

Or is my mind debased by spirit weak,
Too weak to soar in heady regions rare,
But sinks to wallow in a paradise
That fools devise to play their silly games?

Or is my mind the probing, timid cry
Of fearful, mortal flesh that seeks to brave
Its doubtful way through awesome universe
Where seldom seems to tread the very God of it?

Beyond

The Stars and I

I do exist, I live and breathe awhile
Upon a planetary speck that orbs
Its journey tentative among the stars
That throb with lifeless energy of life.

The Course of Life

The youthful years of life that rush along
In endless days of warmth and happiness,
Give way eventually to somber shades
Where patiently abides in confidence
The thought of death, the pallid shock to life,
While every roseate illusion flees
The frantic grasp of consciousness and leaves
An ashen face to ponder death's demands.

John Niemirovich

The Thread of Life

"My children, my children," he sighed, "my children, my children,
Begotten of those begotten in endless skein,
The common thread of life entangling all
In challenges that try our very souls.
 You give to me, in innocence, your trust,
Anticipating guidance through the world.
Think not I never feel your doubts and fears,
While I, in mortal limitation, strive
To look into the future yet undawned
By looking back into my days gone by
And giving them to you that you may thrive
And carry on the tangling thread of life.
Be not unduly saddened when I chide,
Nor must I not expect your just chagrin,
For would a father chide his erring child
When he himself was chid by harried sire,
Unless it be to show the ways of life.
Let not my anger brief eclipse my love
That ever shines to guide your fledgling days.
To all, my love; I pray you doubt me not."

Beyond

Vagrant Stirrings

When all the loves sustaining disappear,
When they are stripped by time and circumstance,
When I am left to roam the world alone
And know that no one waits for my return,
Where will I go to fill this emptiness
That aches, though now I have those loves?
Perhaps the twain of time and circumstance
Will prove compassionate in years to come
In wearing away those aching yearnings strange
That seize my heart with sadness now and then.

Familiarity

The countless ages continue rolling by
Unfolding, for a moment brief, events
Which quickly fade and, withered, fall to null
To blend into the world from which they sprang.
Events so numerous they overwhelmed.
Now minds, whose innocence did marvel once,
With surfeit reel into complacency.

John Niemirovich

The End

Waste not your time in vain regrets when life,
Whose incremental force ephemeral is,
Asserts no longer its vitality
Amid chimera abuzz with tales of fate
With tallies stern that list the deeds you've done
Or left undone in careless days gone by.
Despite the fearful wish to stay your doom
There's naught to do but patiently await
That last event immutable decreed by fate.

Faith

Be not naive in searching for a friend,
A friend to trust in stormy days or calm;
Seek not perfected folk, for none there are,
Not here on earth, beyond the cradle.
The cradle, that haven of innocence from which,
Into a seething world of endless strife,
Betrayed by sin to grief and care, we fall.
Be not naive, but don't surrender faith.

Individuality

The puzzling universe is spread before
Inspiring wonder that, with all the time,
The lavish riot of time that nature flaunts,
That we from limbo's depths are borne to see
Its timeless mystery for moments brief
Which form our individuality.

Beyond

Through Death

I thought of fearful death,
Was fascinated by its gruesome task,
Its unconcern for dignity,
Its stark inevitability.
As time went by I saw through death;
Through death I saw a face of beauty rare;
I heard its voice which softly spoke
In tones of tenderness,
"Return to me, return to me."

The Riddle

Constrained are we
Within our destinies,
Enduring lives
Decreed by fate
Who
In awesome majesty,
Imperious to all our doubts,
Commands
With absolute relentlessness.
However stark this view,
Consider how,
In spite of all,
We nurture deep within
A driving dream to understand our plight,
To push away the darkening night
Which shades our genesis
Wherein resides the riddle.

John Niemirovich

Generations

The face you wear is not unlike the kind
That formed man's picture in my mind,
Your thoughts and feelings though have me confused;
Have I grown old and fallen so far behind?

A Dream Dissolving

The biosphere with seething life doth teem;
The stars are burst and formed anew to gleam
Within the cold and limitless expanse
While fragile man bestirs within his dream.

Vanquished

Devoid of sanity, devoid of reason,
Devoid of hope and trust, devoid of love,
Devoid of what his destiny proclaimed,
Yet deep within there clings his deathless soul.

Sally

I looked on you as just another problem spawned
By forces fanciful and far beyond my ken
Until I saw your frozen features melt in tears;
How beautiful and strong were you, how cruel was I.

Beyond

Photographs of Dreams

Some photographs of people appear so charged with life
To turn away were something lost; to stay this loss
I gaze upon their pictures till it seems we touch
Then shy away from an intrusion bold and rash,
A harsh dilemma that chafes with fascination,
But one which brings to view the gallery of man:
The photographs of youth have eyes that peer with hope
Into a future filled with all the dreams of man;
Their visions streaming through from boundless, fearless mind
Impart a glance of dazzling, penetrating light
That easily turns aside the wary, weary world
Which gladly to its youthful promises defers
Anticipating something better, by and by.

The middle age shows a picture furtive eyed
Intently watching hectic days go swiftly by
With apprehension born of clashing dreams that strive
To mold chaotic worlds to one utopian.

With eyes that look perforce within, the later years
Are pictured soft within the gallery of man;
No more the face attempts to hide the hopes and fears
That vie to win the heart of man, but wears instead
The mystery bestowed by nascent understanding
As deep within, the waning entity, which dwells
Behind the face serene, confronts its vanished years
To view again those airy dreams that tantalized,
And more than that, to muse upon the why of dreams,
Those gossamers that populate the worlds of man.

John Niemirovich

A Being Apart Within

I see within my probing consciousness
A being infantile that lives apart;
An entity that seems more dream than flesh;
A being far beyond my touch and tears;
A being tossed, abused, reviled, denied;
A being mortal striving gallantly
Who must alone decide his fate while I
Can only gaze and marvel on his struggle.

To Church

Do those who stay from church do so to taste
The wrath or love of God while those who haste
Let those ordained endure the task of faith
While they await their former state replaced?

A Pause

In expectation tentative and vexed
It waits its genic task to consummate
To pass to time the generation next
This cell that soon may flow through cervix' gate.

Beyond

This Place

What place is this, I wonder where I am?
A place I see so clearly with mine eyes
But which confounds me through and through
With sparkling gems of understandings
Within a void of darkness nurturing doubt.
So many colors blended artfully
With forms that range from awesome majesty
To lithesome, delicate, intangible exquisiteness.
Intangible too its scented flowerings.
Intangible—so it is— its essence rare,
Its airy essence, that of which I seek.
The dross through which I move in ceaseless search
Is no whit less intangible than that I seek.
This dross of substance flows from earth to form
Then back again as earth itself will flow.
Within this flow, my consciousness, aware
Of ceaseless flow, aware and ever seeking,
Aware and never resting in its quest,
The source and destination of this flow,
The essence of this flow, its mystery.

John Niemirovich

Dreams

A dreamer's dream is wistful make believe
Conceived his nagging doldrums to relieve
Within the greater dream reality.

Alas, these dreams of bliss are brought to life
Accompanied by the spectrals gaunt of strife,
Reflections of the dream reality.

And who can say a nightmare's pain is less,
When felt within the shade of consciousness,
Than that inflicted by reality?

Or disillusioned schemes less drear to bear,
When choice is trapped in harsh dilemma's lair,
Than stern denial of reality?

But will his schemes of practicality
To bear his dreams to actuality
Appease the behemoth reality?

Beyond

Myself

He seeks, you seek, I seek; but seek we what?
"We seek ourselves," we say, with deep concern.
Yet in the stillness of my awe, I ask,
"What will I see when once I find myself;
What if the self I find is not myself;
What if the self I seek is buffered from
The essence of reality by sheaths
I call emotion and my intellect;
What if the self I seek is self-perceived
And not reflected of a greater truth?"

To Each His Destiny

We each must go our separate way through life
Though when we start our doubtful trek
The fear that haunts the dark unknown before
Constrains our eager steps to walk with those
Whose presence buttresses our frail resolve.
The genuine response we feel within
Endeavors to complete a bond of trust,
A trust that bids us share our inner lives;
But all seems vain, we find, as passing years
Discover that the bond is tenuous
And each must live perforce his destiny.

John Niemirovich

Thoughts

I thought of you with constant expectation,
I fashioned images of joy and bliss,
I held you tenderly within my mind.
To learn the essence of your being ethereal
I plunged to maddening depths of concentration,
But suddenly you slipped away from me;
I tried to reestablish our intimacy
Yet knew our past association gone,
A severance decreed by other thoughts.

An Enigma

I feel within myself an entity,
A being quite apart from this veneer,
This tangible person known to you and me;
This entity waits in darkened haze
Though rarely felt or heard, and never seen.
But is this whispering and ghostly voice
The distant call of waiting reality,
Or clever madness disguised seductively;
Will I succumb to falsely promised joy
And run berserk with mad anticipation,
Or quietly pass with dignity of faith
Unto the land of which the ages speak?
Be kind if madness should usurp my mind,
For such as this bespeaks a worthy quest.

Beyond

Of Thee and Me

O, I, of flesh and blood, am cognizant
Of my awareness of my earthly life
And ever wonder if all I see is all,
If all I see and feel is really so,
Or just a blurred illusion seen in dream?
Am I an entity among this mass
Of entities who are so much alike
And differ mostly in an ego's whim,
A whim that thrives or perishes as all,
And ruminates, as all, of thee and me
Or am I but a transitory thought
Within an awesome, endless happening?
This difference, it seems, appears to me
As real as thee and me as now we are
But sinks to plumbless mystery when I
Would peer to matters dense and absolute
Which lie beyond a fog impenetrable.
O, I, of flesh and blood, am sore confused.

John Niemirovich

It Is Spring Again, But Where?

The grass was greening, tiny leaves unfolding,
The air was crisp and clear, the sky was blue;
A stirring deep began within myself,
A stirring vague and distant, as though it held
No promise of better days to come
But rather, dulled and tarnished memories
Of younger days of living hopes and dreams
That blossomed of and for themselves and not
For future days of joy ad infinitum.
Amazed, my mind was seized with troubled thoughts
As on I gazed and felt elated not.
Why not enjoy the sights and sounds of spring,
The elements were all conjoined with verve;
Were they somehow diminished by the years,
Or had the zest of life forsaken me
And left me with a mass of aimless thoughts,
Confused, and lacking songs to sing of spring?

With Love and Hate

In coexistence love and hate entwine
As stymied love with caring anodyne
Is oft rebuffed by forces prevalent
That seem to emanate by hate's design.

Beyond

Dawn

All through the closing night in fitful sleep
I sought repose in restful slumber deep
As imps synaptic, wild in frenzied glee,
My psyche did harass till sleep would flee.
Now dawns another day in sunshine bright
Illuminating my room with magic light
That chases darkness chimerical
Conceived by doubts and cares inimical
That haunted yesterday and vied all day
To track each step I took till down I lay.
Yea, troubled nights are difficult to bear;
How quickly, though, the sun can banish care
And reinforcement of resolve employ
To reinspire the daunted will to joy.

Mystic Depth

I felt embraced by fears of life and death
And fought depressing chills that coursed throughout.
Succumbing not, but reeling fearfully,
A moment brief of welcome peace obtained
When somewhere from the mystic depth within
There came to me revealing knowledge that
There is no sadness drear beyond this now,
Nor is there known the fear of loneliness.

John Niemirovich

From Then Till Now

Do you remember, Time, when I was young?
Although it seems so very long ago
It's nothing but a moment, more or less,
Since I was young and squandered precious hours.
But days are running short and vistas bright
That stretched to future days beyond my sight
Are greying now that age is somewhat schooled.
So swift the hopeful days from then till now,
The journey ends in sore perplexity.
So fleet my time on earth, familiar stars,
That drift for eons through the dark of space
Seem solidly attached to nothingness.
I am ephemeral, yea, but through it all
A witness to an awesome mystery.

The Mind

Insatiable, the probing mind of man;
It ever strives unknown to known to span.
Not pressing care propels it far aloft,
But dreams that dare the universe to scan.

Beyond

Bones

Upon the plain of life are scattered wide
The bones that carried laughter, hope and tears.
Where dwells that loving laughter dear to heart?
We known the tears are dry to flow no more,
But where in all the universe can be
The hopes and dreams that stirred those quiet bones?

The Sky

The colored photograph was captioned thus:
Andromeda Galaxy in distance lies
As measured by the flashing speed of light
Two million and a quarter years from here.
But where in heaven lies Andromeda
Since all those years of never ending flight
Has carried it from there to God knows where,
Along with all the other twinkling stars?
With heaven's furtive motion all about,
How plain it is to see, without a doubt,
The sky we see is that which used to be.

The Mystery of Life

How dominating the mystery of life.
How patient, silent its profundity
In waiting to enfold us at our death:
How deferential its care in dooming us.

John Niemirovich

Biblical Man

Is that the face of god I see so near
That tugs my heart for love in name of God
But turns away the proffered love of God,
Confounding all the virtues sweet of life
By nursing deep within an endless doubt,
A doubt engendered by a distant sin,
A puzzling doubt of anger, fear, and shame?

Paradise

A dream has man, a dream of ease and wealth
Within the world which bears and nurtures him.
His fertile mind devises tools and means
To realize the mundane schemes he dreams.

A dream is paradise, a shining dream
Persisting in man's mind through ages dim.
But how shall man attain to paradise,
An airy dream beyond his mortal grasp?

Body Chemistry

If body chemistry will prompt a smile
Though those that smile have never met or touched
What force unseen can be the catalyst?

Beyond

Pedagogy

When teaching children examples of adults,
How they for good or bad fulfilled their day,
There always is the danger insidious
That they will learn the deed and not the lesson.

The Ocean's Edge

While walking on the beach one sunny day
I looked beyond my worldly cares and saw
The ocean wide receding from my sight
Into a glare of dazzling white and gray.
Around my feet the mighty ocean teased
As on the sand it fell in foamy sheets
And playfully came bobbing to the main
In never ending, splashing, tireless waves.
Entranced, I gazed upon its liquid mass
Attempting there to see the lure that calls
The brave, the greedy, and the desperate
To sail their ships upon its heaving tides.
I heard, instead, a host of distant lands
Whose siren call is sung within the lull.
The song of lure is heard within those breasts
Whose restless spirits dare to answer Fate
Who beckons them to sail the ocean wide.

John Niemirovich

My Words

My words are thoughts that fly upon the air
The vocal messengers of silent doubts
That burn within the crucible of life,
That struggle endlessly with puzzling clues
To fashion individuality
Within the awesome, teeming universe.

Tomorrow

The shield protective borne by instinct's care
Is meant to turn aside today's alarm,
But only intellect nurtured of dauntless hearts
Can lay the plan to foil tomorrow's harm.

Mortality

How fearful and unsure is man's mortality,
How fathomless the spreading universe,
How tiny seems the teeming planet Earth.
Has man been blest or curst with his mortality?

Necessity

Necessity the mother of invention is.
As man devises means to ease his burdened life.
Survival, too, demands its complex burden eased
So bears the child necessity of intellect.

Beyond

The Wash of Time

The many forms expressed of fecund life
Which touch the fleeting, shifting shores of time,
In evolutions balanced flow and ebb,
Imprinted are in layered, durable rock
That will in time erode and wash away
To form another sedimental tome.

I Thought I Knew

A new morality revealed itself,
While secretly I thought of this and that
And passion flowed in wild imaginings,
This complex body frail is not my own!
Then what I am, and what I am to do
Is still a tantalizing mystery.

My Goodness

Sometimes in retrospect, complacently,
I think that I have wisely picked my course
To travel safely through the frays of life
(And so I must to bolster my esteem).
But there will be a day, which fate has picked,
When all the knowledge that I command
Will pall before the host of circumstances—
Of age or accident — that spells my doom.

John Niemirovich

The Sun

Upon the distant, circling planet earth,
The unapproachable sun, an awesome orb
Of massive size and blazing energy,
With tempered light engendered fragile life.

Through time evolved within this fragile life
A pulsing nerve of feeling, knowing sense
That lends its energy to intellect
Which dares to dwell on all including sun.

This Path They Walked

They walked along this path in years gone by
Absorbed, no doubt, in busy wonderment
Of what their day would bring of joy and care.
They walked to all the goals that life demands:
To work and play, to love and hate, to death.

This path is walked along but seldom now,
For time and need have commerce elsewhere set.
It seems a lonely path bestrewn with rubble,
Neglected now, but not without its memories,
For here have tread the busy feet of those
Who walked along this path in years gone by.

Beyond

Muses

The artist and the arts are briefly one
As momentarily the muses deign
Their grace shall touch upon the artist's brow
While all time else the mortal artist yearns.

The Flame of Love

The artists flame of love but briefly burns
As now and then his muse his suit returns
And deigns her grace shall touch his barren brow
While all time else the slighted lover yearns.

John Niemirovich

One World

The many nations of the world were formed
When primitive man withdrew from wandering
And spent primeval days in seeking ways
To learn Dame Nature's ruthless discipline.
But now is man much more than savage force
Contesting other tribes and other life
For finite space upon the planet earth.
Instead, evolved has man to stewardship
Of all that lives upon the planet earth.
It lies within his power to decide
What form of life shall live and what shall die
As more and more he cultivates the earth
To feed his population burgeoning.
The impetus of nationality,
As seen in history, will ever lead
To give and take upon the battlefield
Unless mankind agrees to other goals.
No easy task is his to curb his pride,
To empty all the caves of ignorance,
To wean all doubts till trust is mutual;
But forge man must one world with dignity
Where men may live in peace and man survive.

Beyond

Memory

As insubstantial as a breath of air
Within a howling storm is mortal man
Who disappears to nothingness no less
Should fame and fortune smile upon his days
Or fail to count one second of his life.
The being of man, the form of which he is,
Although appearing durable, ephemeral is.
Then whence the will to fashion airy worlds
To conjure lengthy ages gossamer
That briefly live in hectic, frantic strife
To linger only in our memories?
And why is memory, the unseen guide,
The wispy link from now to yesterday,
As durable to last all ages past?
Impressionable is memory of man;
It readily records the sheerest event
And builds an ever expanding consciousness
Which is the present sum of what he is;
Should it collapse, so too the world of man,
And he and all his schemes would then become
Remembrances in search of memory.

John Niemirovich

Tears

I wonder if those tears that streak your face
And mellow hardened hearts as down they race
Are sad concern for fate of missing friend
Or ego's plea its sorrow to replace?

Maelstrom

Upon each passing day I bend my eye
And wrap myself within its comfort sure
Convinced its preordained successor bodes
A world secure to keep away all harm;
But every now and then a timid glance
Will dart beyond my safely ordered days
To catch a fearful glimpse of timeless night
Wherein a ruthless maelstrom tosses me.

Beyond

Nocturne

Alone at night in slumber's soft embrace,
Awakened by a flitting, ghostly dream
I toss and turn in seeking sleep's sweet grace
And hear afar a rare and pleasant theme.

Its soothing sounds from dreamy limbo rush
Becalming fretting doubts of darkest night,
This lonely song I hear in midnight's hush
As it and I are borne to peaceful flight.

The song is sung by raucous iron wheels
And roaring whistle, filling all the sky,
Of lumbering train, as through the night it peals
Which distance mellows to a calming lullaby.

Intellect

Our intellect is borne by force of life,
As such its incident is far beyond
Our mortal will to have or not to have
But must perforce exist by greater force.
This force of intellect can we but hope
To harness to the principles received
From inspirations awakening.
This aweful force through nature's whimsy can
Be turned to do unto ourselves the things
The very things we do unto our world.

John Niemirovich

Which Path to Follow?

Would you a straight and endless path prefer,
A path that never once returned your steps
To pass among familiar sights and sounds;
Or one of circular design that curbed
Your steps to travel evermore within
The sights and sounds you know familiarly;
Or would you step from circle to circle
In constant search for sights and sounds unknown
When once each circle's sights and sounds are known?

Innocence

How many times have you experienced
The heat of feeling foolish when you thought
That you had acted childishly naive
And bared to all the world those trusting ways
That stern sophistication ridicules?
Belabor not your burning sense of guilt
Beyond the point admission and resolve;
What you have felt is haunting innocence,
The remnant rare that long ago was found
In those who once abode in paradise,
Which disappeared in aweful cataclysm.
You may be cognizant of this milieu;
You may delude yourself that you are there,
But doubtful is the chance that so it is
Until that grace is once again enjoyed.

Beyond

The Rest Remains

One day a man of fashion strolled into
A haberdashery a tie to buy.
How greatly taken aback was he to see
A single selection displayed upon the racks,
A thousand, more or less, he estimated.
So populous but so unwanted too.

Trend

We constantly review the images
That ever populate our consciousness
Rejecting those we hold in low esteem
As not in keeping with the latest trend,
But something quaint and hopelessly passé.
The images we raise to prominence
We hold as markers to a proven course
That show the way that life is traveling
And swear within ourselves that this is truth.
Imagine our surprise when once we find
The universe has quite another mind.

John Niemirovich

Night View

The closing night reveals a wondrous sight
Which blazing day confounds and hides from view,
A blackness strewn with softly shining stars
Whose distant light entices us to yearn
To soar aloft among their magic fire
To learn the meaning of their splendid charm.

O, Who Am I?

Unique am I, as individual,
Who have these many centuries endured.
Each instance of my being separate
From all the others who, as I, contend
With universal forces to survive
The mortal days allotted me.
The reason for my here and now unknown
Except through tantalizing wisps of faith.
Each smile of mine like yours and yours and yours,
Each tear, each thought, my birth and death like yours.
Essentially like you in all respects
And yet apart from you in mortal garb.
The many centuries go rolling by
And still I ask, "O, who; O, who am I?"

Beyond

Circumstances

The solace some enjoy when circumstances
Removes their lot from days abject and drear
Is viewed by those unfortunate as pride
Till they themselves are blessed with happiness.

The Force of Life

Amelioration notwithstanding
The natural force controlling life holds sway
While we its elements manipulated are
And fearfully endure its bidding stern.

Paradise Recalled

I once recalled my days of innocence
When every step I took upon the earth
Enthralled my soul with nature's rhapsody
Whose song I heard in praise of all as one.
Then stole upon my heart the chill of fear
As clearly came to view the distance wide
The busy passing years had carried me
From nature's trust and comforting embrace.
I saw that separation is current coin
That man must pay for life within this world
As crowded days demand their growing needs
And every want confounds his promised joy.
But though my heart was sad my spirit rose
To pray that all was not forever lost
That once again would live my days of innocence.

John Niemirovich

Different Routes to God?

To those of you who don't believe in God,
Who coldly search for something never known,
And those who seek in sorrow something lost,
Will all one day convene at journey's end?

A Robin Sang

I saw one day in spring a robin sage
Upon a leaning tombstone gray with age
Who sang of love and life in tireless flow
Unmindful of the sacred peace below.

The Two of Us

Within us lives two persons side by side.
Impatiently the world demands the one;
The other we insist is really we.
The world demands and we submit or else
The world, the sum of all our social selves,
Despises and rejects our stubbornness.
The one will dance to any merry tune,
The other grandly moves to sacred tones
And ever strives the fiddler to confound.
Determined to survive as individuals
How warily we consume our earthly days
In standing guard against our social selves.

Beyond

The Mountain Climber

I know so well this valley spread before,
Which busy hands have groomed with loving care.
Its life engendering bounty swells my breast
With love and thankfulness for all it gives;
But when I look beyond these rolling hills
And see the stark and snow clad mountaintops,
A restless force within responds to them.
A force that looks beyond the things I know,
And I am drawn perforce to venture forth
To gambol high among their loneliness
In search of their elusive mystery.
The search does not diminish their allure,
For always when I look to them I feel
Their beckoning in equal intensity.
In equal measure within myself I find
A strength of spirit and of flesh that dares
To climb on high with mountains towering.

John Niemirovich

A Window in a Squall

Upon a hill I stopped to gaze awhile
At clouds so low they nigh on touched the ground
And should have darkened all the world about
Except for atmospheric whim that tore
A segment from the gray and misty mass
Which let the setting sun shine through
In yellows pale of soft, appealing hues
While in their midst there trailed sheer wisps of white.
It seemed a radiant window of grand design
Revealing hills that rolled beyond my sight
That else were hidden beneath a darkened sky.

The Fabric Sheer of Life

Upon this bursting globe are souls in billions.
We fit in every nook and cranny known
And ever seek for those as yet unknown
Destroying links of life along the way.
Where once the grass and stately forest grew
Are miles of shifting sand and burdened land,
Where once rivers ran with water fresh
Are poisoned streams besmirched in senseless haste,
Where once the ocean's vapors fell unspoiled
Are killing drops of burning acidity.
Make hast we must our actions to relent
Before the fabric sheer of life is rent.

Beyond

The Stew of Life

Through diligence of effort have I found
Another fear with which to plague myself.
The fear of death with gruesome images
Is standard fare and not my newest find.
The latest fear I dread is that of life,
But not the view of tribulations drear
Which check our lives at every step and turn.
It is the view of human form composed
Of cells attached to form my flesh and blood,
Of interrelated organs here and there
Whose functions tentative my tenure binds.
From this concern there springs another doubt,
Allowing perfection of this milieu,
If choice were tendered, would I choose or eschew
To live all time within this fleshy stew?

This Body Mine

This body mine to which I an confined
Is it the Prodigal of Paradise
Or manifestation dross of stern decree
That cast mankind from Eden's rarity?

John Niemirovich

I

A tiny speck am I immersed within
A limitless expanse of space bestrewn
With matter stirred by boundless energy.
The self I see is matter formed to flesh;
Each thought I think is spawned by energy.
The universal elements are here
Contained within a smaller mystery,
Infinitesimally a particle of
A universe which has the wherewithal
To look upon itself and wonder why.
As one among the universal host
I gaze upon it all and wonder, too;
Complex and huge it strikes my understanding
This awesome apparition engulfing me
Of which I am as much a part as stars
That fill the sky with dazzling multiplicity;
And always burns within my mind a spark
That yearns to probe the darkest shadows cast
And seeks the greater, guiding force unseen.

Appearance

From time to time it seems that I have changed,
That I am not the person that once I was,
Especially within the minds of those I know,
Although I know full well, in spite of doubt,
That I am still the same, the very same.
The change is of ascendancy of parts.
The parts of which I am composed take turn
As one is predominant anon another.

Beyond

Words

If those who seek are drawn to read herein
What I with pen have measured of my thoughts,
The words that they will see will never be
A semblance of the vanished, airy being
Who made these marks in days that are no more.
The concrete now of what will be their time
Will search in vain my person to compose.
How like the riddle of life that words should be
More lasting than their fragile authors wee.

Reality

What apparitions familiar do I see
That mask a system fragile to extreme?
They look to me and I to them with eyes
That do not see for they like glass transmit
The energy of light to nerves within,
Yet still within this breast of mine do they
Evoke what I and others choose to call
Our thoughts of love and deep concern for those
Who look to us with eyes that do not see.
They speak to me and I to them with words
That momentarily ripple unseen air
Then tentatively take unsure abode
Within an unendurable entity.
What deep and hidden force is true reality?

John Niemirovich

The Individual

A quandary: how numerous we are,
The individuals of species sapien—
As those of all the other species here,
And those that long have disappeared, as well—
A teeming population dying to live,
In vicious struggle, that each may realize
The tenuous right to live awhile.
Our commonality is rationalized
In disciplined and searing humility,
And failing that, mere madness rounds our day
As ever closer looms the mystery
So near to reach but never touching us.
The master plan we ever strive to read
But must content ourselves, in lieu of this,
With contemplation of contingencies
And consolation spiritual that
The lonely, frightened individual
Though insignificant essential is.

Beyond

Here and Now

I might, as Omar said, observe that we
From regions quite unknown have sprung to view
To interact with one another here
Til love and hate are spent and we are gone.

The pool of genes that swim through time and thigh
They say is traced to fecund slime bestirred
By crashing bolts from gathering clouds of mist—
A meld of matter and crackling energy.

But where and how the source of breeding buds
That made the thee and me that interact,
And why and where the end to which we wend;
An awesome mystery our view confounds.

Revelations

Our struggle to survive demands so much of us
We fail to see that others, too, are caught
As deeply in the universal struggle.
Their dignity, the sum of their resolve,
Is all we see upon the moment met,
And it is only through reflective thoughts,
Which analyze dispassionately,
That we descry the passion of their lives.

John Niemirovich

Flowers

As surely as the plants abounding lush,
From tallest tree to curving blade of grass,
Am I another brief expression of
The mystery inexorable of life
Which sallies forth amid a hostile place
To blossom soft and warm in frozen space.

The Struggle

Upon this planet Earth endures a struggle,
A struggle to determine dominance
In both the basic form of instinct's strife
And passion's higher quest for freedom's weal.

Unexpected Joy

Among the many cares and woes of life
Along have come, when in the throes of care,
For reasons far beyond the understanding,
A time or two that fills the heart with joy;
Though small and unimportant those events,
They were indeed a glimpse of happiness.
Though happy then, those moments dear to heart,
Which were engulfed in stifling care and woe,
How strange that their drear ambience should prove
Too sad to feel again their vanished joy.

Beyond

Human Spirit

In spite of flaring passions now and then
How quietly courageous is the human spirit
In yielding to Dame Nature's demanding will
To whose decree's we are subservient.

The Eastern Island Lament

By stars and inborn restlessness their days
Are strung into a life of wandering.
Beyond the hazy curve they seek their goal
Til on this island small they come to rest.

But now their lust to seek new land is spent
And here in aweful isolation fast
They live their lives in carving men of stone
That rise above their desolation drear.

Upon the sea they turn their massive backs
Perhaps to shun elusive thoughts of faring on
And burning, bitter sighs of plans unwise
To venture forth from ancient haven safe.

"Come see, come see," they seem to say to whom
May travel on the lonely, silent sea,
"Come see my plight and take me on your way
That I may leave this lonely spot of land."

John Niemirovich

Speculation

How many million years it took to leap
Into the space of earth I do not know
Nor do I know how long my wait to reach
Beyond the stars that ever meet my gaze.

But where the challenge lies will I be found
For I am being bound to speculate,
Who must expand my restless consciousness
Until the universe and I are one.

Our Galaxy

Our galaxy, I hear, is spiral shaped
With trailing arms that hold a host of stars
A dazzling pinwheel huge against the night
That spins upon the breath of God's command.

Beyond Ourselves

I lived awhile upon this jolly earth
And pondered every facet of my life.
I thought of kith and kin and strangers, too,
In search of that essential force within
That ever touched my heart with loving pain
And learned how little we are beyond ourselves.

Beyond

Irony

The more I hear of all who came before
The more it seems how minuscule am I—
The present teems with millions trampling dust
That represents the hopeful ages past.

The Transition

A presence felt but just beyond my sight
Yet though I seek both high and low for it,
In every nook and cranny within, without,
The secret force I seek is unrevealed
And nothing greets my senses other than
The very things I see before me now.
It must be there in form invisible,
Or could it be within the things I see,
The things of life that lie before my way?
Then these are what I must investigate.

The Whale's Return

Land ho! I spy the main.
It lies but just ahead.
Come on, you lads,
Upon my lead,
The beach, from where we sprang
So many eons past,
We soon shall make.

John Niemirovich

The Versifier's State

They looked for beauty in truth of life
To give a meaning to their lives that else
Were spent in fighting fearful doubts and pain,
A search that led them nowhere from this place,
For all we ever find is that we are,
And here is where we must forever be.
Reality has truth and beauty for all
Except who opt to stay in darkness' thrall.

Is Love So Shy?

Is love so shy it must remain aloof
In secret depths to hide our feelings soft,
Not from cold malice ever hovering
But fear of pain accrued to ego? Yes!

The Ghosts of Yesterday

Devoid of substance's contentiousness,
The ghosts of yesterday before me loom
As wispy remnants of their former flesh,
The lusty vestment cladding present time.
Both they and I—though they without the voice
To yea the dreadful point, yet wish they might,
And rather would forget than labor it—
Both they and I agree no easy task
The frightful human saga to endure.

Beyond

Shards of Man

With steps of hope I travel back and forth
Across the land in search of greener fields.
So small my steps that I must strive to see
What lies ahead, thus seldom find the time
To think of all the things I leave behind.
So great my zeal to see what lies ahead
My past recedes from memory, while time,
Which cloaks in mystery my distant past,
Reveals to later generations a puzzle
Of common things which I have left behind.

When All the Multitude

When all the multitude have one become
When all have realized that all are one
In all the many conceited differences,
The bonds of ignorance shall fall away.

Imperious Parents

I see myself with an intensity
That more than not beclouds the larger view
That I am child of fate and destiny
Imperious parents stern of all the world.

John Niemirovich

The Way of Words

How difficult it is to understand,
To sort and analyze the rushing stream
Of images that overwhelm our minds.
How welcome to our equanimity,
Like paths between whose bounds we trust our feet,
Those strings of words that we by daily use
Arrange in narrow boundaries strict
To guide our doubtful, erring, fearful sense.

Certainty

With clarity of pain that leaves no doubt
I clearly see what time has done to you,
What fleeting time must do to all of us,
Of some who seem to leave by far too soon
Who leave so many things undone, unsaid.
I search the features worn by care and pain
For semblances I knew of yesterday.
How sheer their fleshy delineation
That flee so quickly to withered age
Now stripped of all the force and tone of life
But not of love, my love, but not of love.
So thus must we, the very last of us,
To withered age and realms unknown beyond,
Our thoughts and steps constrain to wend,
For leave we must with absolute certainty.

Beyond

A Finger Snap

Time, time, and time again I ask of Time,
O Time, of what complexity art thou,
Art thou an essence of the universe?
And Time will answer me, from time to time,
In such and such a way, if time he has—
If but my endless pestering to stop:
"And what request of Time have you, this time?
Perhaps a Jovian view of me will do.
Know, thou, that God has endless power?
That by this very essence He may choose
To snap his finger, if so it pleases Him,
Proclaiming that as His finger snaps
A universe from void He will create
And long before the snap has died away
A judgment day convene, if need arise?"

In Beauty's Praise

When first I knew the miracle of life
I longed to sing in praise of all its charms
Not realizing till many years had passed
That what I felt was poetry divine:
The song was being sung and I had merely come,
From God knows where, to thrill to beauty's praise.

John Niemirovich

The Flow of Time

This house in which he shared his wedded life,
Where all his children grew into adults,
This house of memories that keen the heart,
This house—but now no more, but now no more;
For younger eyes upon it gaze and see
Not memories but dreams of what shall be.
How strange that memories are born of dreams
That only see the far horizon nebulous.

The Restless Force of Life

The restless force of life consumes itself
As form replaces form in slow and steady change,
In endless competition doomed to strife.
In slow degrees ascendant forms emerge
So slowly that today's appearance seems
The only world that could and should exist;
But change it does and that which changes not
Is often left behind the vital pace,
Imprinted fast within the pages of
The layered archives of the shifting crust
While that which changes lives before our eyes.

A Maddening Dream

A maddening dream recurs spontaneously.
It deftly crowds all thoughts and memories
And constantly dominates my feeble regrets
With jealousy I should have felt for you.

Beyond

I Greeted Spring

I greeted spring with somewhat less the verve
Of former years, but lo! the sum of years
Since first I saw the light of day is such
I wonder not forsythia's yellow paled.
The dogwood's bloom I see, as now bestirred,
Belatedly, my senses are—this early day in May—
Is brilliant white and pink seductive soft
Upon the spreading lawns of beckoning green
While at their feet azaleas sumptuous
In iridescent hues profusely flower.

Suitable Lore

The odyssey of man through ages vast
Is charted by accumulated lore
Whose matter all engrossing is, to wit:
The doubt of goals and suitability.

A Bird Am I

From dinosaurs they say we sprang and yet
I have no recollection of this birth
And for that reason I cannot say
Nor nay nor aye to whom my forbears be.
Upon my feet they would you bend your eye
And there espy the claws of yesterday.

John Niemirovich

Hate

Insatiable is hate as e'er it seeks
To feed itself with more and more of faults
That convoluted are from simple facts of life.
A raging, roaring fire that must be fed
Till love and life and trust are quite consumed.
So great the heat of hate its flame attracts
The restless gaze bemused of all the world
While soft, abiding love in silent sweetness grows.

The Management of Space

Swift time,
The phantom streaking through
The pages of our life,
Is charged to manage space
Allowing thus
Events infinite
Within a finite world.

Reason

Though all the world say nay, the mind will probe.
Though other minds be closed, the minds of some,
In strict obedience to nature's law, will probe.
The universal force that powers reason
Will find expression spite of doubts and fears,
In spite of ignorance and repression.
Today's taboos standing drear and stern
Will fall dissolved by reason analyzed.

Beyond

Away

He looked upon the world with wide-eyed wonder,
A tiny locus of trusting conceit
And groundless expectation—quite undone
When sped away his world without his leave
For fate had not decreed that in his time
And in his place a major act evolve.

Death and Life

Is death the all of life,
The end of every act of man,
The constant over the shoulder eye
That either cares not or knows not
The pall it casts upon the mind of man?
Is death thus far removed from life
That life and death are poles apart
And life might have a realm beyond the reach of death?

John Niemirovich

Conceit

And when I die
Will I
In regions void of all I knew
Bewail my doom
As on I wander through
The endless space
Of my imagination
Or will there be
A resolution
Beyond my understanding?

The Energy of Life

The energy of life
Outstrips by far
The quantity of matter here on earth
Hence life upon itself must feed.
Nor can the management of time
Employ its policy,
Mortality,
To sate life's appetite.

Beyond

The Lee of Life

Infinitesimal though this moment brief
Replete it is with those activities
That shape the restive universe:
Energies enormous interacting with
The massive matter spread throughout;
From second to second an expenditure
Of energy incomprehensible;
Yet here we stand amid the lee of life.

Splendid Attitude

How magnificent the attitude of many,
How ethereally they transcend the dross of life
Their spirit shining through with endless splendor
Where one expects the dreariest to prevail.

The Loss of a Loved One

She goes to where I dare not, can not tread,
But how my keening heart bewails her loss.
Her memory intensifies my grief
As painfully and slowly I defer to death.

John Niemirovich

Yesterday

Remorse: a gnawing, sorrowful review
Of vaporized events that nevermore
May gather in reprise to hindsight's redress;
Alas, I would I could have held them fast.

The Hand of Time

Hush, the universe is all about
And through it moves our fleeting lives uncertain
Upon the hand infinitesimal of time
That sweeps infinity relentlessly.

Upon the hand of time we ever move
Till days are one and only puzzles remain
Of what we are in spite of what we think we are.
We dare to think but not without our doubts.

Beyond

The Force of Life, a Test of Faith

Upon this planet earth, the force of life,
Arisen from genesis as yet unknown,
Endures as entity incomprehensible
While species ephemeral one another devour.
No right nor wrong nor moral sense to stay
Its course relentless in feeding upon itself,
No tearful sentimentality impedes
Its ruthless self-perpetuation.
In dire consideration of life's design,
Where only stoicism pervades, I ask,
Wherefore those tears that sear the eyes of man;
If life itself cares not for man, who does?

Father

Here stalks the specter grim embracing one I love.
Familiar features once I loved are now unknown
Yet still I love the fatally afflicted one
And would myself embrace and tenderly protect
This one I love from death's unswerving finality,
A vain conceit from one whose time is just as brief.

John Niemirovich

Autumn

The forest floor was strewn with leaves sere brown
    and curled
Which rustled underfoot as on I walked within.
I wondered why I felt this force compelling me
To wander through the starkness left of summer's flight.
'Twas death I saw, the death of summer's lush refrain,
But in that loss I sensed the pulse of life to come
And comfort took that such a flight as this were one
That might as boon be granted to the likes of me.

Motives

I wonder where they are?
I do not seek the snows of yesterday
Nor its roses red,
Though they are also gone beyond recall;
I seek that which was rarer still.
I seek the motives moving men and women
Through busy, troubled lives.
How rare that they should labor daily
When all their tears and sweat
Would pass away to nothingness,
How rare the hopes and dreams relayed.

Beyond

The Mystic Bond

How can the morrow be unborn
When all that is or all that is to be
Is now within the fabric of the universe?
Can anyone a single thread addend?
The now and here is all there is;
It but remains the knowledge to acquire,
The mystic bond of time and lore.

Undisclosed

I bide here waiting, waiting ever waiting,
But waiting for what?
It surely not is death
For that I know must come
Regardless of my expectation.
Then what is that for which I wait,
What force unseen with stern decree unvoiced
Demands I spend my life
In waiting, waiting as here I bide?

Ideals

What force within constrains my eye
To seek a never to be found ideal
Within the host of those whose paths and mine
Are fated to be met?
Why seeks my mind unreal demands?
Is this the force that shapes the world?

John Niemirovich

There Something Lies

There's something more to man than flesh and blood.
There something lies beyond his sinewy appearance—
A wraith which hands can never touch,
And always just beyond our sight.
It hovers there untouched by time and grief;
Though flesh decay, something still commands respect.

The Setting Sun

The setting sun of fiery red that sweeps
Its russet colors through the western sky
Is merely relative to axial spin;
But as I peer across the rim of earth
I cannot otherwise but think there surely is
A God this glowing spectacle devised.

The Clock Within

The clock within in harried measure beats
And we encourage time this pace to match
That we may hurry to the next event.
When all events allotted to our life
Extracted have the essence of our beings
We wonder why so swiftly passed our time.

Beyond

The Span of Man

Too short the growing season,
Too soon the leafy canopy is seared and underfoot,
Too soon the song of summer ends,
Too like the span of man.

The Now of Life

How strange the now of life
Reflecting past events as vague illusions
Though they were once the now of life. If life is thus
    illusory,
Then where in all the universe
Is there a harbor for reality?
Is that the why and wherefore of reality;
The mind's creation to infix illusion,
A reference firm to steady life?

The World Defanged

No fangs, no claws, no horns, no thickened skin,
No simian arms to climb to leafy haven,
No swiftly moving thighs to leave behind
Primordial hunger ever stalking prey—
Yet man survived by dint of intellect.
Now paused in doubt and awe he contemplates
The ever burgeoning task to hold at bay
This convoluted world he has defanged.

John Niemirovich

Lovers

How foolish lovers are; they put their world,
Their world entire, into a pair of eyes
Then languish breathlessly in maddening doubt
To see the look of love within those eyes.

A Taste of Wine

Think not, in vain complacency,
A satisfying draft of life to quaff,
For life is not a banquet laid for mortal taste.
Contrarily, 'tis life that feasts upon the likes of us
Who only may the tiniest sip imbibe.

Mementos

The photographs
And fond mementos life bestows
Quickly fill our cluttered lives
With precious memories;
Tenaciously they cling
Until imperiously
Our deepest emotions they command
While only waiting dissolution can
With stark finality release the bond.

Beyond

Dreams

What force unseen controls my mind subconscious,
What force decrees my sleeping mind shall wander
Through ghostly corridors of spectral events
Conceived within the soundless depths of me
Without the wakened yea or nay of me?

Those We Love

Each one of those we love must steal away
Whom jealously in silent expectation
We guard with wearying confrontations;
We love to love but hate to hate that love
For life without that love were desolate.

The Legacy

We are the sum of all the ages past,
For good or bad the legacy is ours
Of all the hope and schemes that went before.
How little we add to all that has accrued,
How difficult our merit to preserve,
Bespeaks the debt we owe to long ago
Which labored on with less of lore to guide.
And now our time has come to leave our mark
Upon the present page of history
That those who follow fast upon our steps
May similarly criticize the past
For surely criticize they shall if we
Bequeath to them the legacy intact.

John Niemirovich

In Retrospect

I wandered o'er the quiet countryside
In search of those who made the sights I see:
The barns and houses faded now with age
Whose springhouses low amidst the shade still stand,
Who cleared the growing fields and pastures broad
And fenced those hard won fields with sifted stone;
I do not know why here my heart was drawn,
I only know in retrospect belatedly
That sadly those were here I sought are gone
And nevermore upon this earth will toil.

A World Beyond

A lasting fascination turns the mind
With equanimity to ponder that
Which lies beyond the reach and touch but not
Beyond an inner spectral conjuring.

A distant gaze, an enigmatic smile
Proclaims the mind's preoccupation with
A lonely, mystic world unpeopled, yet
Replete with happiness and endless promises.

Beyond

Sorrow

What happens to the sorrow felt on earth
When to the heavens fly those salvaged souls
Who privileged are to reminisce on high
In jovial nonchalance of past events?

Is sorrow merely here today as we
And when consumed, a shadow doomed to wander
Amid the hazy halls of memory?
But, O, the many mortal pangs that shadow bears.

A Place to Be

Is there a being rare or otherwise
That here on earth or far beyond the stars
May truly exist without a place its own
But here within the fertile mind of man?

Within the mind of man are beings born
Who unsubstantiated live and thrive
Insinuating deftly their lives with his
Without the slightest hint of measured space.

John Niemirovich

Above All Else

Mysterious is death as also life
Advantage though to life, for it we know,
What though in nonchalance we squander it,
While death as yet is still the factor x.

A grief of scalding tears is certain-death,
A fear to be adroitly parried till touché;
But certain-death among all else is sad,
To see the endless stillness now of life.

Genetic Pool

When we appear unto this teeming world
And wonder where, before the shock of life,
In limbo's unremembered realm we bode,
'Tis plain to see we've swum the sea of genes.

In

That life devours itself 'tis plain to see,
But why to dogs and cats are cattle fed
Had e'er perplexed and bothered me until
I saw that cats and dogs are in and cattle not.

Beyond

Constrained

I've climbed to lofty heights from time to time
To gaze upon the tangled world below
And seen that none are free from life's constraints,
That all must bear the burden of its doubts.
I've seen that this enlightened view is that
Which should prevail within a world of reason
But cannot long sustain the rarity
Demanded of this lofty view and sink
Within the teeming mass to take my place
Amidst a shrinking world of do's and don'ts.

On Viewing Tombstones

They sleep the everlasting slumber well
These lads and lasses fair who once of yore
Embraced the trifles and tragedies
That made their world their very own and which
Bequeathed thence have now become our own.

John Niemirovich

Evolution

Through eons leading to the present time,
The helix splits and readjusts itself
In concert with compelling laws of life.
A rigid sequence, clove to flesh and blood,
Demanding close agreement to its train,
Exacting dire consequences else.
A binding contract forged from stellar dust
By forces far beyond our minds' conceit,
A humiliating, maddening, rousing denouement
And yet, although obtuse its purposed end,
Whate'er the ease its durance to forget,
Responsibility we must endure.

Beyond

Ancient Roads

There once a wagon went this way
In ages past of long ago;
It carried folk to festival
To celebrate the joy of life;
It carried them to congregate
In prayerful meeting, there from God
His help and comfort to beseech.

A rutted road the wagon's way:
To field and grinding mill it wound,
To turnpike wide and highway dry,
From there the world to woo or war.

These teamsters long have gone their way,
Their fervent thoughts are silent now,
Their wagons turned to dust by time,
Their ancient roads macadamized.

Ah, Spring

Ah, spring, the echo soft of life's first breath.
Can life have been so wrong to issue forth
With all its caring, crying twists and turns
When here in farther, cooler latitudes
Its annual reemergence, spring, bestirs
With velvet tyranny the vaguest heart
To bask within its joyful mystery?

John Niemirovich

Of Love and Other Things

I do agree there's something more to life;
There's something gives us goals to contemplate;
A shadowy substance ever tantalizing
Which will seduce the fervent individual,
But tie the tongue of those who dare to meet
As ever it hovers so near but out of reach.

From Dawn Till Now

A vicious world consuming body and soul
Till some were wearied to distraction's verge
And refuge sought from endless, killing strife
With words innocuous—or so they thought—
Which civilized proxies were to crushing blows
Allowing peace to soothe their harried souls;
And thus was born within their wearied minds
A verbal foil, the word delusion hight.

Starkness

How many trifles have I collected close,
How many niches filled had else been vacant,
How many shields to ward from view
The paucity of life's requirements?

Beyond

Trivia

How oft are memories, that painless lie
Within the fast embrace of time forgot,
Evoked, without the least permission granted,
By unexpected trivia mundane?

How dear these trivia that usher forth
Those precious memories unwanted but
Entwined so close we can't of them conceive
Apart from us and ever yield we must.

Goodbye

Goodbye begets a lingering regret
As fast constrained within the fading past
A special relationship, by increment
Of lasting cares and pleasures formed,
Is now denied to us by stern decree.

No longer living in our hopeful breast,
The love we shared defers to memory.
We stand perplexed and sad at loss of touch
As to the awesome, universal expanse
Departs our personal love to meld.

John Niemirovich

Order

In order for disorder to occur,
Some order must have previously been;
And since disorder cannot orderly be,
It cannot be that chaos rules the world.

Amen

Whatever spurs you on and fills your days
With myriad thoughts, and hoped for excellence,
In contrast with all other choices viewed,
In ghostly retrospect the time will come
When you will see your many days
Within a wisp, for which you've spent your life.
But worry not; you've done your best; amen.

Beyond

Prostrating Prostrate

I heard the test results and thought:
I need more time.
I have so many things to do.
It's not as though I've been remiss;
I've really been involved in many things.
I'd like to taper off,
But only after I've tired myself unto exhaustion.

A multitude of needs and deeds I tallied,
As on and on I rambled,
Until within the depths of me
A vagrant wisp of hope I conjured
And nurtured desperately,
But all to no avail
As ever so gently death responded, "Ha".

Wearied Caring-Love

It doesn't seem fair that we should learn to love,
That we should learn to feel and ache and need,
That deep within a yearning should arise
And grow to banish from ourselves ourselves,
That we should value those of endless need
Beyond the caring of our own concerns.
Could we but see beneath the mask of those
To whom we dedicate our every breath,
Pray, would or should we free ourselves from them,
If so we could—but no, we carry on.

John Niemirovich

Cosmic Commensuration

What speck of dust is this that searches deep
Within the labyrinth of consciousness
For what he is and why he came to be.
The smallest part divine the cosmic whole?
But wait, perhaps there's something to the lore:
The longest journey's end might not but be
A step away. Perhaps man will persist
Within the narrow bounds of sanity
To thwart his own destructive bent of mind
To journey through the centuries till
His bits of knowledge are commensurate.

Flicker

How sobering the span of time we have
Compared to that the swirling cosmos spends
In rearranging endlessly the meld
Of energy and matter infinite.

The births and deaths of stars are commonplace
As we beyond ourselves inspect the skies
While here on earth our restive tenancy
Within this panorama is but a flicker.

Beyond

And God Made Man

You've fallen short, so what? You think to be
The creature fanciful you've generated
Within your dauntless, searching mind? Perhaps.
But think how far you've come by dreaming on:
You've reached beyond the mortal bonds of earth
To seek the manifold design of God.

Destiny or We?

Do we control the twisting course our lives
Insinuate through puzzling destiny
Or merely adapt our desperate conceit
And grudgingly accept the proffered choice?

Forever Alone

If you could live forever and never lose
That searching zest your knowledge to increase,
What would you see along your endless way
But endless death and woe and tearful eyes?

And would omniscience eventually gained—
If none were near with friendly, loving smile—
Be worth the absent praise of those not there
Whose old esteem your endless trek induced?

John Niemirovich

Grief

You grieved for those who went before;
When you then left, to be with them, I grieved amid
my solitude
Until I found another love
Who grieved when death consoled my grief;
And so it is, and seems always,
Our destiny, this grieving world.

Mother

Of sin I've heard and seen the grief of it.
How best to rectify the errors chosen
Can only by our Lord be finalized:
By punishment or annihilation sure.
A timid, doubtful voice, howe'er I raise,
"O Lord, the grief of death it seems to me
Is punishment enough for such as we."

Beyond

Charmless People

You say they lack the charm of warmth, but O,
There still remains the question unresolved
Of who and what we troubled mortals are
And why we fare amid the universe
Consumed with right and wrong and purpose vague.

They furl their brows and wander off aloof
No doubt aware of charmless destiny
And of those charming people fortunate
To be submerged instinctively in ease.

Compensation

I saw an ancient hothouse bare of glass,
A weather-beaten frame and nothing more,
All grown of weeds in riot of negligence;
I thought that that in sorry plight the end
Of someone's erstwhile bustling, hectic dream.
I wondered why our world should so uncaring be
As weaving life and death with ruthless hand?
I reasoned then that this for all to know
Bespeaks ameliorated mortality;
For who can doubt the joy of dreams come true?
Minutest compensation some are sure to say
But let them also say what otherwise shall be.

John Niemirovich

Benefactress

Within a fantasy I saw a girl
As happily she moved along in dance;
This way and that she turned in silent rhythm,
For music not a single note I heard.
Upon her face, when once she turned my way,
I saw a smile that every darkness drear
The nether powers ever proffer forth
Were vanquished effortlessly by its charm,
By confidence within her peaceful eyes,
As she were here to banish care and woe.

Loss

To die at any age is grievous loss,
To die in youthful bloom pains doubly so
For youthful death seems death of life itself
And not the weary end of life's travail.

The Tilted Earth

The middle of winter, snow and ice abounds,
The days are short; the nights are cold and long,
The somber hills bereft of living leaf,
No trace remains of petals soft and scented,
The frozen ground belies the song of summer
Yet deep within that cold and sparkling frost
Abated lies the germ of yet another spring
Awaiting but the orbit of the earth
To tilt the hemisphere beneath the sun.

Beyond

Twain

Why is it that our grief of scalding pain
This stifling, overpowering burden, grief,
Assuaged by time meandering and faith enduring,
Is from the refuge amelioration seen
As an experience of beauty and reward
Devoid of which our lives would empty seem;
Are grief and love the one and same;
Is grief the echo unbearable of love?
If that, then how profound this awesome twain.

Death Wish

Mortality, how subtle, allowing us
To savor life with but a thought of when,
With final exactitude, you claim your due.
But though aloof and quietly abiding time,
Yet emanating darkness taints some hearts,
Who, learning futility, despair of hope,
And deep in contemplation, e'er unvoiced,
In sheer obedience consign their lot,
To stay your stern rebuke, by wishing death.

Fear of Death

As life's cessation, death itself conjures
No fear within the analytical mind;
But that within which pictures images
Of ghastly states unknown and dire, frightens.

John Niemirovich

Madam Caprice

And thus a multitude of intimates
Have stayed awhile, which for some pleasant time,
And hopeful, too, were in her dreams ensconced,
The fondest e'er she dared to conjure forth,
Until the banal day she saw how far
Her finery anticipated exceeded
The promises her beaus proposed to her.

Fantasy Pursued

Suppose a fantasy, a vaporous conceit,
Were all that held a soul and body intact
Whose bond were else dissolved in hopeless plight
As harsh reality consumed the will
To meet the daily challenges of life,
Would fantasizing thusly constitute
An aberration better not pursued?

Unbidden

To my surprise did I discover that
My fear of life and death is so profound
It reaches not a solitary tear,
It quivers not a single fleshy tissue,
Nor furrows momentarily a frown,
Concedes a sigh, unveils a doubtful glance,
Especially at rest amid the dark,
The universal hush of deepest night,
When thoughts and doubts unbidden confront my soul.

Beyond

Happiness of Yore

I wonder now and then of yesterday
And think how fortunate and happy those
Who dwelt amid the fabled time of yore
Till omnipresent care beclouds my view.

J. S. B.

Upon hearing certain of his music, arose
A feeling sad, forlorn, devoid of hope,
Nor saw I happiness among that host
As somber specters glided to and fro;
I paused in solemn contemplation drear
Despairing ever of understanding how
Such sadness beauty's charm conveyed
Until I realized 'twas not morbidness
That trailed behind the pen of this composer
But beauty rare as seen through mortal eyes.

John Niemirovich

A Twist of Fate or The Will to Survive

What makes the world go round?
I mean our lives on earth, and not the planet earth.
My net is hurled to snare,
Perchance, an answer hidden deep
Within the lore that life bestows:
The will, ingrained instinctively to survive,
Appears most obviously in the cast.
But what is this demanding to survive,
Is it a fear of death?
Do trees and germs consider death
And thus react in horror to survive,
But how?
And thus it seems,
Perhaps,
That death does not enliven us.

Beyond

Time and Memory

Unto our midst in swirling perspective,
Swift time decrees and rushes myriad events
That ever so briefly engage our heart and mind
Before receding far beyond our reach
When we are left to ponder their import:
Events, both sad and happy, once departed
Demand and receive our full respect.
Yet no amount of searching ever brings
To pass remembered ghostly events that once
Substantial seemed beyond the bounds
Of dissolution—durable, tangible.
Yet in our minds a corner waits to store
As memories events that once were real.
And thus it seems that memory alone,
That timid and uncertain trait of mind,
Can challenge time, the behemoth supreme.

Vagaries

Was I, as puny as I am, to stave
The wicked world in which I found myself;
Confused of purpose, awed, and wholly unable
To choose my way through countless vagaries?

Regret

It is as surely impossible to say and do
The words and deeds that life's commitments demand
As surely it is, on looking back upon our lives,
To not regret not having consummated them.

Where?

Before the dawn of day,
Before my time,
Where wandered my soul?
And when the sun shall set,
And I may never marvel more,
Where wanders my soul?

Friendship

For some the lure of friendship brims their hearts
With joy whose limitless horizons
Offers pleasures which conceal unflattering
And troubling views that chill the heart,
And proffer challenges heroic instead
Of sunny carefree days; Yet some there are
Who love and dare endure those troubling views.

Beyond

Temporal Steward

Dame Nature, stripped by chilling frost and wind
Of summer's cooling green and autumn's blaze,
Forlorn appears as fast in slumber's embrace
She dreams of all the many season's past
And those to come. Full well she knows they shall,
For what upon our spinning earth orbiting
Can stay one whit her yearly blossoming
If all the world her loyal steward persist.

Salvation

If animals, e'er wandering furtively
Through many eons, are merely fleshy pawns
Enslaved through instinct endlessly to bear
The edict only to live and reproduce,
There is no thou or I in wildernesses,
Only coded actions and reactions harsh;
And men were well advised to seek salvation.

John Niemirovich

Awesome Fire

How many stars uncountable reside
Amidst each blazing galaxy so removed
Their blinding lights are wearied to naught
Before their journey brings them nigh
Where man must peer through glass to see their glow.
How many galaxies seen and unseen
With some so distant that their speeding rays
Have just begun to touch our orbit's path
While some so far they may expire unknown.
What power unimaginable must be
That rules and regulates this awesome fire
Which conquers frigid darkness absolute
Then nurtures blossoms caressed by breeze.

Dame Justice

Dame Justice stands in view of all who care,
A scarf around her eyes to isolate
Her partiality to stay complaint;
A balance poised to register
The sheerest evidence of wrongful acts;
Within her hand a sword demands respect
From all who challenge her authority—
Or does the scarf, in melancholy truth,
Betray the Dame's desire injustices,
Which shamelessly abound, to hide from view?

Beyond

Memory and Thought

What thought can issue forth from deep within
Our questioning and ever seeking minds
Without the reference of memory
That teeming repository wherein resides
The witnessed sum of all we have become.
The persons real and what they have endured,
The fleeting phantoms of our fears and hopes,
The measured facts that rule our doubtful steps,
All stored within to shape our thoughts.
The mind impressed by textures, sights, and sounds
Relates and rejects until emerges thought.

John Niemirovich

The Antiquity of Now

I think of now as what I am
But I am not the child of now,
Today is not my genesis,
My birth goes back before antiquity;
So far removed am I from what I am
I never shall it seems determine that
From which I sprang
Or when or why or what I have become.
And yet I think and feel
With equanimity and surety
As though I sprang from now
And all before were just as now
But if that were
What need have I of questioning?

How fine the increment
How long the subtle transition
From then till now,
That I cannot recall.

A blank that barely bears
A blurred impression
Of races lost in ancient times
Is total sum of what I think I am.

Beyond

Mayhem

How stunning the image of eyes so clear
They seem to manifest the soul within,
The facial features regular, untouched
By hate or fear, the laughter confident,
The bearing of innocence—this all
Engendering a disbelief in sanctity,
Suspicions that all is merely sham facade,
A seeming revelation to some who yield
To harbor secret monstrosities.

And Then There Were None

Beneath a brilliant blue and fleecy sky,
In bursting exuberance, undeniable Spring
From winter's chilling grip unfetters herself:
The fertile fields are plowed, the distant hills
In speckled green adorned with budding leaves,
Both tentative and tender, seeking sun
And rightly fearing anticipated frost;
Shy dogwoods, virginal in spotless bloom,
In woodland bower stand decorously;
Alert and watchful deer, their hunger past,
Through flowing grassy surfeit gamboling;
In mauve profusion wild geraniums;
Overhead in rising thermals buzzards soar
With silent, effortless meandering
Reminding all of springs that won't arrive.

John Niemirovich

A Quiet Rainy Day

Down, down, down the rain,
The ceaseless pattering on pane and roof,
The misty veil insinuating everywhere
Till all is lost in mystic gray;
Ephemeral streamlets flowing by
And frantic puddles lashed by pelting drops;
The damp pervading chill
As patiently I yearn to see the sun.

The ABC's of Pictographs

I look upon the world as even you.
But you and I have mutual understanding;
If only others more removed from us
Could think as you and I and all our kin;
To prove my point, consider, if you will,
These walls adorned with hewn and painted forms,
From these we choose the morrow's hunted prey,
Which even strangers cannot fail to grasp.

Beyond

Memories

Of places, people, and dates are memories:
Unique encounters placed upon the earth
Whose motion through the cosmic void
Removes its locus ever from that place
Whose fleeting time can never beat again
Nor hold again those persons as they were
Upon that day so very long ago,
Or moments past, it matters not;
In memories alone encounters live.

A Violent Genesis

Tectonic plates against each other grind
Unleashing deadly waves that shock the earth;
Some, meeting one another, enfold their crust
Where mountains wondrous rise to frigid heights,
While others plunge to angry molten depths
Then spew their spleen volcanic o'er the land.
Though underneath tumultuous the earth—
In shaping land and sea—its handiwork
Of mountain, plain, and valley brings to view
A panorama irresistible
As mollified by the most delicate,
Most mystifying view of nature's force,
The irrepressible incidence of life.

John Niemirovich

Thanksgiving

From nature's store enjoy we all we have;
Do not in haste undo her ancient lore.
The food we eat came not in packaged form
But slowly culled from wilderness's realm
By generations of endless laboring
The killing wants of life to mollify.
If all that man through centuries has culled
And nature's store through eons evolved
Were thrown away through man's mismanagement,
From where, if all is lost, to start anew?

Another Story Ends

So, here at last are you. How long the wait.
How many times throughout the years have I
Anticipated how you should appear,
What guise upon your visage, warm or drear,
And whether you should tender prove or harsh?
I must admit that not with lightsome heart,
But rather stoically, awaited you
Have I, O Age, O Ancient denouement.

Beyond

Faith

If there is life beyond this life on earth,
And I believe there is, if life beyond
Is on a par with that of Eden lost
Then why the poignancy within our hearts
For this a temporary, fleeting world,
A place of trial, tribulation, and tears?

This world, it seems, is not our heart's desire
But merely tenancy entitling us
A cherished glimpse which now and then we view
Of all that was and may again return,
A fleeting glimpse to test our faith.

Moments Rare

How capture moments sweet whose essence rare
Prohibits touching them which rather touch
Our hindered hearts in fashion mystical
And then reside but in our memory
Where ever and ever they tantalize our days?

The Soul

The soul, its mystery, its shining strength.
How feeble the vessel holding the precious wine,
How unbelievable that those we loved,
Though weakened by age, yet how enduring shone
The precious gift of life that seemed so close
But now has gone to only God knows where.

John Niemirovich

To Know or Not

We would, we should, that we could always see
Beyond the faces placed before our eyes
To look into the very soul of man
To see his worst intent or highest hope.

But would we, should we be content to know
The darkest secrets hidden deep within,
The highest, brightest passion burning bold
Within the breast of those who are as we?

The Puzzle of Life

Why me? Why have a multitude of woes
Descended heavily upon my breast
To burden me beyond the human curse;
But yet again, of all the multitude
Who could have lived and shared this life with me,
Who never limbo's nothingness escaped,
Who never mused in pondering this puzzle,
This subtle, intriguing, chary-yielding puzzle,
I ask and wonder why this privilege rare?

Sanity

If we were not by local problems plagued,
If we were free to concentrate on views
Which show our minds the world's immensity,
If we could see the world's complexity
What should we do our sanity to guard?

Beyond

Understanding

When God to humans would confer his thoughts
It should as no surprise be learned he speaks
In ancient terms which all can understand
And thus precludes misunderstanding doubts.

The Lasting Mystery

Another day has gone away fore'er,
Another day has brought and solved its share
Of petty problems wrapped in petty pains,
Yet, see, the lasting mystery remains!

On Growing Old

Though youth would much prefer eternally,
With features e'er unmarred, his realm to rule,
Yet patiently, in distant years, awaits
A ghostly faded visage strange to eye.

A chance encounter with a vagrant image
Reflected from an unexpected looking glass,
One stressful day, presents this visage pale
To those whose youth but lingers on in mind.

Now reigns confusion drear while youth recoils
To steel itself to face its future found,
Then wonders why on earth it tarries more,
Confined in that which harbors youth's demise.

But wait, the spirit moving youth rebels,
For it does not to years or care submit
But casts aside its youth to dwell with age
To bide its time until its fated end.

John Niemirovich

Despot's Price

Now chaos rules where once an iron fist,
In velvet fantasies, controlled and crushed.
Don't sound the pool genetic—swirling froth—
Its depth has stained the land in tragic waste.

The talent born to govern dared to speak
Within a stifling storm of fear and hate,
It paid the despot's price with pools of blood.
Now must we wait for nature's remedy.

The Finite Universe

If truly finite is our universe,
As on and on its mystery expands,
It surely must by nothingness be bound
Since nothing lies beyond its boundary.

Although composed of nothing, nothingness
Must surely be possessed of measurement
By virtue of its having received with ease
The roil of matter stirred by energy
Which then, by gravity conformed and whirled,
To massive stars with satellites condensed.
How short, I wonder, of infinity
Does nothingness extend, and what beyond?

Beyond

Beyond Fate

That feeling rushing one from life secure,
Away from all familiar social mores,
Becomes a forceful wind engulfing one
And pushing one as if the merest straw
Throughout the whole of one's allotted life
While one submits to that which fate demands
Albeit seemingly of petty value.

Persistent Yesterdays

Of mores and manners current yesterday,
But unremembered presently by most,
Uncalled-for memories have cunningly—
Past watchful eyes of fashion's jealousy—
Insinuated fast within their minds.

With eyes that clearly see today's event,
While inner yearnings hark to yesterday,
They wander seeking not that which they see
But those elusive ghostly images
That populate their errant expectations.

John Niemirovich

Crowded Reality

Intelligence and life's reality,
An ancient marriage, some aver; howe'er:
The crop of fantasies engendered by
The fertile field of our intelligence
Grows rampant crowding reason's budding thoughts
Of justice, fairness, truth, and tolerance
Till they must struggle to survive
In darkened, tentative environment.
And therein lies the wispy paradox,
An endless quandary stirred and muddled by life
As our intelligence creates apace
A host which crowd from view reality.

Apparent Infinity

Where ends the present day which now we know
And then begins anew the morrow's day;
The moment last of minute or of second,
Or tenth, or hundredth, thousandth, on and on,
Until infinity denies the dawn?
But wonder not for these divisions end
Upon a time coincidentally.
And yet there are divisions infinite!
And so infinity enclosed within
A finite event infinitesimally is.

Beyond

Spring and Daffodils

Forsythias ablaze in yellow finery,
Magnolias alluring all with white and mauve,
While daffodils await the slightest breeze
To dance their silent mirth at spring's rebirth.

Of a Fragile Shell and Extinction

Suppose this body frail in which we dwell,
In which we interface the universe—
A place expanding far beyond our sight
And filled with stars beyond our reckoning—
Suppose this fragile shell of brash intent
Which seeks to understand and leash this world,
This mortal cell we know and call ourselves,
Suppose it merely is another choice
Of evolutions never ending task
Of casting circumstances apropos
And we its earthly living breathe of God.
Then who we are, that inner brightening,
Is more of worth by far than what we are;
For surely was a day when what we are
Was not upon this earth. Then is it wrong
To think of days when what we are is gone?

John Niemirovich

Almost Paradise

Nostalgia's tender touch upon our hearts,
Unbidden, unexpected, subtly keen,
Demanding ever its presence contemplate,
Departing quickly into nothingness
Before analysis unravels it.
This very mystery have I of late
An inkling of its genesis determined:
A fleeting glimpse of that which might have been,
A rare unveiling—almost paradise.

Memory

When that which must be done imprinted is
Upon our ever active, searching mind,
Arising from a normal fear of want—
That this must never unreplenished be,
That this demands correction immediate—
This fear is never brought into this world
Without a myriad host of circumstances
All striking simultaneously the brain
Through eye and ear and other sensories,
Where all reside within the birthing bed,
That place at which the memory is born.

Beyond

Eden

The tree of life, a tree of knowledge rare,
Whose leafy branches held forbidden fruit,
Whose strict decree of sacred genesis
Was disobeyed in cataclysmic pique
On Satan's surreptitious whispering.

"Do not of this intrigued be", said God.
"Behold, of all the gifts that meet your eye,
Be free to know: of this beware", He charged,
"Lest you may think that from your molded loins
Creation sprang, not procreations gift."

An Impression of Sally's Illness

In furtive flight, an object caught my eye—
An oak leaf blown about by winter's blast;
Against the dazzling white and chill of snow
Which once in living green absorbed the sun
And supply waved in summer's welcomed breeze.
I gazed awhile upon its lonely flight
Then sadly went upon my weary way.

A Quandary of Life and Space

Another farmstead populated
Another farmhouse leveled
Another farmbarn recycled,
It seems that change is here to stay:
However more inhabitants convey greater change.
Will we with greater change
Increase or wane?

John Niemirovich

Infinity Traversed

The second hand, which travels round and round
The face upon my clock with tick and tock,
Is harmless, wishing none to irritate,
Though some might find its ticking, tocking so;
Yet when it grows to distance infinite,
Its arc must also infinite become,
And there you have a boiling irritant;
For when it ticks and tocks each second's time,
Its arc infinital must reach in time
The second next (as anyone can tell
Who has impatiently sat and watched a clock)
And this demands infinity traversed
Within the space a finite second spends.

Another Doubtful Day

Yet another doubtful day to face anew;
How easily intentions lose their place
As random choices set our daily course
Decreed by powers far above ourselves.

Spring 2001

Forsythia ablaze in yellow comforting,
A bright oasis in a dreary scene
Of nature's deep and frozen sleep till when
A vivid spring awakens all the land.

Beyond

Youth and Age

The many years, when now in retrospect,
I ponder, surely breathtakingly,
Impressively are startlingly numerous.
For who except those manic moved to tell
The endless chain of daily occurrences
Which strung together comprise our past
Would not be shocked to see the sum of age?
This lengthy panorama assimilated
Which, when I see the doubts of youth, engenders
Commiseration for the trials before
Which I with difficulty have stepped beyond.

Fear

The braggart's flowing claims of courage brash
Denies existence of the specter fear,
Yet fear is here to stay, it but remains
A choice of giving in or going on.

Creative Credit

In disregard of all the killing toil
Of ages past, of blood and sweat and tears,
The crowning glory of governing,
The rule by all of all who so agree,
Democracy, is ever challenged to respond
To those who find its freedom not a gift
But license to deceive those not as they
By referending creative credit's toil.

Title Index

A

A Being Apart Within 90
A Bird Am I 131
A Blushing Flower 3
A Conflict Unresolved, Perhaps 68
A Crowd of One 23
A Dream Dissolving 88
A Dream Is Love 39
A Dreamer's Caution 8
A Finger Snap 129
A Fond Farewell 32
A Girl 67
A Glimpse 23
A Long, Lost Friend Remembered 6
A Lover's Dilemma 49
A Maddening Dream 130
A Mortal Question 71
A Pause 90
A Place to Be 145
A Puzzle of Life 32
A Quandary of Life and Space 181
A Question 2
A Quiet Rainy Day 170
A Rare View 25
A Remembered Idyllic Impression 56
A Robin Sang 114
A Special Face 35
A Stronger Force 79
A Taste of Wine 142
A Twist of Fate or The Will to Survive 162
A Vain Pursuit 36
A Violent Genesis 171
A Window in a Squall 116
A Window Through the Clouds 68
A World Beyond 144
Above All Else 146
Absent Heart 77
Across the Ages 20
Adam Again 72
Adam's Child Unbound 54
Adieu Ingrid 66
Adios 50
After the Promise 42
Again 35
Ah, Spring 149
Almost Paradise 180
Alone Almost 76
Alone at Last 45

Amen 4, 152
An Enigma 94
An Impression of Sally's Illness 181
An Unanswered Question 47
Ancient Roads 149
And God Made Man 155
And Space 16
And Then 14
And Then There Were None 169
Another Doubtful Day 182
Another Story Ends 172
Antagonist 64
Apart From God 29
Apparent Infinity 178
Appearance 118
Autumn 138
Away 133
Awesome Fire 166

B

Babel 44
Beauty 70
Benefactress 158
Beyond 20
Beyond Fate 177
Beyond Ourselves 124
Biblical Man 100
Birth 16
Bittersweet 28
Body Chemistry 100
Bon Voyage 21
Bones 99
Born of Yesterday 25
Budding Spring 56

C

Caprice 52
Certainty 128
Charmless People 157
Christmas 38
Circumstances 113
Commonweal 70
Compassion 36
Compensation 157
Complacency 68
Conceit 134
Confused Desire 43
Constrained 147
Continuity 4, 82

Beyond

Contrast 69
Cosmic Commensuration 154
Crackpot 64
Crowded Reality 178

D

D Day 62
Dame Justice 166
Dame Nature 40
Dark Eyes 42
Dawn 97
Death 17
Death and Life 133
Death Wish 159
Deceit 44
Decisions 31
Departed Friend 13
Despot's Price 176
Destinies 43
Destiny or We? 155
Different Routes to God? 114
Dilemma 65
Distraction 19
Dominance 59
Doubt 64
Dreams 92, 143

E

Earthly Pleasures 37
Eden 181
Entropy 19
Eternity 31
Euthanasia 59
Events 40
Evolution 148
Exposure 22
Extinction 11

F

Facade 79
Fact and Fancy 17
Faded Dream 26
Faith 29, 86, 173
Familiarity 85
Fantasy Pursued 160
Fantasy? 22
Fate 77
Father 137
Fear 183
Fear of Death 159
Flicker 154
Flowers 122

Flux 55
Foolish Dreams 41
Forever Alone 155
Friendship 63, 164
From Dawn Till Now 150
From Dust to Dust 36
From Then Till Now 98
Function 62

G

Generations 37, 88
Genetic Pool 146
Gentle Spirits 74
Giants 19
Goodbye 151
Greetings 80
Grief 12, 156
Guess Who Again? 55

H

Happiness of Yore 161
Harassment 69
Harvest 7
Hate 22, 132
Here and Now 121
Here We Are 14
Hidden Hate 47
Hopes and Dreams 52
Human Spirit 123

I

I 118
I Greeted Spring 131
I Thought I Knew 103
Ideals 139
Illusion 5
Imperfect 31
Imperious Parents 127
In 146
In Beauty's Praise 129
In Retrospect 144
In Search of Me 72
Incredible Remembrances 5
Individuality 86
Infinity Traversed 182
Innocence 110
Insulated Ego 7
Intellect 12, 109
Iris 50
Irony 125
Is Love So Shy? 126
It Is Spring Again, But Where? 96

John Niemirovich

J

J. S. B. 161

K

Knowledge 32

L

Limit 15
Loss 158
Lost Familiarity 4
Love 17
Lovers 142
Love's Delay 42
Love's Venture 46

M

Madam Caprice 160
Madness Accepted 71
Maelstrom 108
Man and Fate 15
March is Here and April Near 80
May 60
Mayhem 169
Mementos 142
Memories 171
Memory 107, 180
Memory and Thought 167
Moments 21
Moments Rare 173
Moralist 24
Mortality 102
Mortals 33
Mother 156
Motives 138
Muses 105
My Changing Love 55
My Dreams 60
My Earthly Life 69
My Faith 41
My Goodness 103
My Love 39, 47
My Love Beyond 25
My Mind 82
My Words 102
Myself 93
Mystic Depth 97

N

Naked Destiny 81
Necessity 102

Night View 112
Nocturne 109

O

O Love 57
O, Who Am I? 112
Odyssey 34
Of a Fragile Shell and Extinction 179
Of God and Man 10
Of Love 75
Of Love and Other Things 150
Of Thee and Me 95
On Growing Old 175
On Viewing Tombstones 147
One World 106
Order 152
Our Distant Love 68
Our Galaxy 124
Our Share of Time 74

P

Paradise 100
Paradise Recalled 113
Pearl Harbor 38
Pedagogy 101
Persistent Yesterdays 177
Perspective 29
Photographs of Dreams 89
Poet 73
Priority 12
Prologue 46
Prostrating Prostrate 153

R

Reality 119
Reason 132
Recompense 66
Redemption 45
Regret 164
Relentless Adversity 18
Remembered Pollywogs of Childhood 50
Resignation 73
Resolution 38
Revelation 70
Revelations 121
Ripples 30

S

Sally 24, 88
Salvation 165

Beyond

Sanity 174
Scribbling 45
Selfish Songs 45
Shards of Man 127
Silence 35
Smiles 38
Social Identity 49
Social Involvement 53
Sorrow 145
Spatial Exploration 50
Speculation 124
Spirit-life 69
Spirits 64
Splendid Attitude 135
Spring 2
Spring 1980 18
Spring 2001 182
Spring and Daffodils 179
St. Patrick 52
Starkness 150
Starry Sky 14
Strung Events 63
Suitable Lore 131
Supply and Demand 13
Surprize 47
Swift Time 11
Swirling Doubts 48

T

Take Care 66
Tears 51, 108
Technology 33
Temporal Steward 165
Thanksgiving 172
The ABC's of Pictographs 170
The Abyss 78
The Actor 10
The Ancient Earth 44
The Antiquity of Now 168
The Beach of Time 1
The Chemistry of Life 53
The Child 18
The Chosen Few 36
The Clock of Life 63
The Clock Within 140
The Course of Life 74, 83
The Creator 59
The Currency of Love 41
The Death of Love 60
The Dilemma of Quest 8
The Dirge of Death 80
The Dream 67
The Eastern Island Lament 123

The End 86
The Energy of Life 134
The Fabric Sheer of Life 116
The Face of Death 78
The Farmer 28
The Finite Universe 176
The First Kiss 41
The Flame of Love 105
The Flight of Light 1
The Flow of Time 130
The Force of Life 113
The Force of Life, a Test of Faith 137
The Game of Life 53
The Garden of Life 67
The Ghosts of Yesterday 126
The Goal of Man 54
The Guiding Force 19
The Guiding Force of Man 58
The Hand of Fate 20
The Hand of Time 136
The Hate of Love 46
The Human Condition or Prelude to Faith 51
The Hypocrite 26
The Image of Man 55
The Indian's Burial 32
The Individual 120
The Lasting Mystery 175
The Lee of Life 135
The Legacy 143
The Light of Day 16
The Long Journey Home 8
The Loss of a Loved One 135
The Management of Space 132
The Masque 30
The Mind 98
The Motion of the Universe 9
The Mountain Climber 115
The Mystery of Life 24, 99
The Mystic Bond 139
The Mystic's Quest 25
The Now of Life 141
The Ocean's Edge 101
The Other Person 28
The Power of Love 20
The Puzzle of Life 174
The Quiet Pat 26
The Reach of Man 3
The Realm of Time 48
The Rest Remains 111
The Restless Force of Life 130
The Riddle 87
The Ruthless World 62

John Niemirovich

The Search 77
The Seeds of Love 58
The Seeds of Thought 74
The Setting Sun 140
The Sight of Mortality 72
The Silent Hills of Leni-Lenape 27
The Silly Goose 65
The Sky 99
The Song of Time 49
The Soul 173
The Sounds of Love 35
The Span of Man 141
The Spirit of Man 37
The Spirit of Spring 15
The Stars and I 83
The Stew of Life 117
The Struggle 122
The Stuff of Love 43
The Sum 73
The Sun 104
The Thread of Life 84
The Tilted Earth 158
The Time Is Now 61
The Transition 125
The Two of Us 114
The Tyranny of Love 58
The Unanswered Question 23
The Uninvited Guest 22
The Unique Commonality 37
The Universe and Man 75
The Versifier's State 126
The Vibrancy of Spring 52
The Wash of Time 103
The Way of Words 128
The Weary Sins of Man 56
The Weaver's Clue 2
The Whale's Return 125
The Will of God 78
The World Defanged 141
There 48
There Something Lies 140
This Body Mine 117
This Path They Walked 104
This Place 91
Those We Love 143
Thoughts 94
Through Death 87
Time 18
Time and Memory 163
Time's Capacity 81
To Be Or Not To Be 12
To Church 90
To Do 81

To Each His Destiny 93
To J. S. 23
To Know or Not 174
To Love 21
To Potter's Field 57
To Tony Niemirovich 1
To W. S. 16
Today Is Not Forever 39
Tomorrow 51, 102
Tomorrow's Child 63
Tomorrow's Time 66
Transit 21
Trend 111
Trivia 151
Truth 14
Twain 159
Two Strangers We 62
Tyrant 65

U

Unbidden 160
Understanding 175
Undisclosed 139
Unexpected Joy 122
Us 57

V

Vagaries 163
Vagrant Stirrings 85
Vanquished 88
Vessels 28
Violent Crimes 29

W

War's Cemetery 24
Wearied Caring-Love 153
What If? 78
When All the Multitude 127
When? 13
Where? 164
Which Path to Follow? 110
Who Do We Think We Are? 13
Why I? 57
With Love and Hate 96
Wonder 1
Words 119

Y

Yearning 9
Yesterday 136
Youth and Age 183